D1569543

Introducing Psychology

Learn the basics of psychology to improve your emotional intelligence, couples communication, cognitive behavioral therapy and to defend from dark psychology techniques

By David Goleman

Table of Contents

Introduction

Congratulations on downloading *Introducing Psychology: How People Think, and How They Can Be Influenced Using Psychological Techniques*, and thank you for doing so!

The following chapters will discuss the basic principles of psychology, and they will help you understand how the human mind works. You will learn the history of psychology and how it evolved into the science we know today. You will also discover the science behind how our brains operate, especially when it comes to controlling how we think and remember.

The book also discusses the science behind how we process emotions, and it looks into ways in which we can increase our emotional intelligence. You will also discover how you can apply your understanding of psychology in order to improve your romantic and platonic relationships.

You will learn about various mental disorders and illnesses, and you will discover ways to deal with such conditions if they are manifested in someone close to you. You will also learn the techniques used in Cognitive Behavioral Therapy.

The book looks at how psychology can be used for self-improvement and the things that you can do to develop a positive mindset in order to increase your chances of success in everyday undertakings. You will also learn quite a bit about dark psychological techniques such as manipulation, and you will discover ways to stop malicious people from taking advantage of you.

There are many books on psychological principles and techniques in the market right now, so thank you very much for choosing this one! Every effort was made to ensure that this book is filled with useful insight that can help improve your life, so please enjoy!

Chapter 1: A Brief History of Psychology

Psychology is the scientific study of human behavior and mental processes. Although the discipline is relatively new, the fact is that there is historical evidence showing that interest in how the human mind works and in what motivates human behavior dates back to several ancient civilizations. Records show that ancient Egyptians, Persians, Greeks, Indians, and even Chinese people were very interested in having a deeper understanding of the human mind. As a scholarly undertaking, psychology traces its origin, for the most part, in ancient Greece.

Psychology in Ancient Greece and Other Civilizations

In its early days, and for most of its history as an academic subject, psychology has been closely intertwined with philosophy. In fact, it was not until the second half of the 19th century that psychology was fully considered an independent subject. Prior to that, most scholars thought of it as a branch of philosophy. If you study ancient Greek literature, you will notice that many of the original psychological concepts, as well as some of the terms that are used today in the field of psychology, were coined by philosophers such as Plato, Aristotle, and many others. These philosophers articulated some of the core psychological ideas—albeit in archaic terms.

The philosopher Socrates came up with a method of learning that was based on the application of psychology, long before the subject was widely understood. His learning method was called "Introspection." To practice it, Socrates and his disciples trained themselves closely to examine their own thoughts and emotions, in order to better themselves and to overcome their mental limitations. Socrates might not have known it at the time, but he was pioneering the use of psychology as a self-improvement tool.

Aristotle, another ancient Greek philosopher, came up with a theory that is known as "Associationism." This theory stated that people's mental activities were influenced by their past experiences. While that may seem obvious to anyone today, back then, it was not common knowledge, and people had many divergent theories about what motivated certain human behaviors.

Ancient Asian civilizations, especially the Chinese dynasties, had a history of administering psychological tests to young people in order to test their intellectual and mental capabilities. There are records that show that some Chinese educators in the 6th century AD used to give a sort of IQ test to their students. They would ask their students to draw a circle and a square with each hand simultaneously, and the results of these tests would indicate each student's ability to focus on tasks and to ignore distractions. Today, many scholars consider this test to be one of the earliest psychological experiments in recorded history.

The human understanding of psychology has not always been linear and progressive—during the Middle Ages, a lot of the knowledge that ancient philosophers had recorded was lost, and most of Europe reverted to non-scientific explanations for psychological phenomena. Those years are now commonly referred to as the "Dark Ages" because scientific advancements in most fields were overlooked, and people preferred pseudo-religious explanations for various phenomena.

In the Dark Ages, people assumed that mental illnesses were caused by demon possessions, and instead of trying to help mental patients or psychologically disturbed persons, they would try to cast out their demons, or they would sometimes ostracize them from their communities. In some communities, people with mental illnesses would be subjected to "witch tests" where they would be tied onto rocks and thrown into rivers (the expectation was that they could use their sorcery to float). We bring this up because it is important to understand that without a scientific understanding of psychology, it is easy to make wrong judgments about those around us who may need psychological help, and we could end up victimizing them in the process.

The following are the main pioneers of psychology as a subject in the modern era:

Wilhelm Wundt and Structuralism

Wilhelm Wundt is considered the father of modern psychology. He set up what is now considered the first psychological laboratory in Leipzig, Germany in the year 1879. Wundt is mostly known for pioneering "Structuralism." Structuralism is a field of psychology that is based on an understanding of the basic aspects of human consciousness.

Wundt theorized that consciousness was different from human thought. He taught his students about the basic structure of the human mind. According to him, the human mind was made up of several elements, most notably thoughts, past experiences, and emotions. Together these elements made up consciousness.

To study the elements of human consciousness, Wundt would ask his students to practice something called "Objective Introspection." That means that they would try to look at their own thoughts and mental activities in an objective manner. For instance, Wundt would ask his students to hold various objects in their arms, and they would then have to tell him everything that they felt as a direct result of holding that object.

Wundt's experiments may not sound that impressive, but he was the first person ever to try to introduce objectivity and measurements into the study of psychology. He believed that the human mind functions by combining "objective sensations" with "subjective feelings."

William James and Functionalism

William James is another notable pioneer in modern psychology. Like Wundt, James believed in the existence of the conscience. Unlike Wundt, James did not think that it was possible to study the human conscience. For James, consciousness was an ever-changing thing, and it would be futile to analyze it. He believed that studying consciousness would be like following someone's train of thought — it changes constantly and unpredictably, so you the information you would collect would be of no scientific value. Instead, of studying "consciousness," James thought it would be more constructive to study "applied consciousness." In other words, he chose to study how the mind allows humans to function in the real world.

James is one of the founders of a field of psychology known as "Functionalism." Functionalism is defined as the study of how the mental processes of an organism can help it adapt to its environment. James believed in Darwin's theory of natural selection, and he believed that human consciousness was meant to help humans to survive within their environments. He believed that elements of consciousness were developed and passed on to new generations (either through teaching or genetic heredity) and they would ultimately become part of a person's traits.

Functionalism is still useful today, especially when it comes to explaining our preferences for exhibiting certain nonverbal cues and body language signals. For instance, both humans and animals to avoid confrontation use the act of avoiding eye contact.

Sigmund Freud and Psychoanalysis

Freud is by far the most popular of all the pioneers in psychology. It is not uncommon to hear about him in pop-culture. We refer to him in common expressions such as "Freudian Slip." The first thing you need to know about Freud is that he was a medical doctor, and he specialized in the treatment of mental illnesses. He was an Austrian neurologist of Jewish heritage. He did most of his work in Vienna, but he later fled Austria to escape the Nazis. Today we know him as the person who pioneered psychoanalysis.

As a neurologist, Freud figured out that his mental patients could not be treated by physical means because their problems were not physical in nature. He concluded that his patients' problems were in their minds. He tried to understand what motivated his patients to take certain actions or to behave in certain ways.

He came up with the concept of "unconscious motives." According to Freud, these motivations drove people towards certain behaviors and tendencies. Although these motivations existed somewhere in the minds of individuals, they were not accessible in the conscious mind. Freud postulated that people have certain desires, which conflicted with social norms and established rules, so those desires had to be hidden deep within the subconscious.

Freud theorized that his patients pushed their threatening urges and desires into the subconscious in order to conform to the expectations of the societies they lived in. This is a practice called "repression," and it is one of the most talked about concepts in psychology and psychoanalysis. He believed that when those threatening desires tried to surface in individuals, the conscious mind would work hard to keep repressing them, and that was what caused nervous disorders in his patients.

Freud also emphasized the importance of early childhood experiences to the mental state of his patients. He believed that people developed personalities in the first six years of their lives, so if a person had a significant psychological problem, there was a high likelihood that the problem started during his or her first few years.

Unlike Wundt, Freud believed that most of what goes on in the human mind is unconscious and that in every person's mind, there is an ongoing conflict between the impulses, wishes, and urges that the person has. This theory is the basis of "psychodynamic thinking," which is still used today by clinical psychologists. Freud believed that human behavior was driven by a need to satisfy one's own desires in ways that were socially acceptable.

Behaviorism

In the 1900s, a new generation of psychologists can along, and they sought to put an end to the arguments between the followers of "structuralism" and "functionalism." One such person was John B Watson, the founder of "behaviorism." Watson believed that there was no objective way to tell what was going on in someone's conscious mind. He believed that psychology should focus on "observable behavior" instead of trying to understand the conscious mind.

Watson thought that if behavior could be observed using scientific methodologies, it could be modified. He believed that people could be completely influenced and conditioned by external events. In the same line of thinking, Watson also postulated that individual choice was a complete illusion. Consequently, Watson believed that people behaved the way they did because they were conditioned to do so by events that happened to them in their past.

B.F. Skinner also subscribed to the behaviorist school of thought, and his biggest contribution to this tradition was the addition of the concept of "reinforcement." According to Skinner, people could be trained to behave in a certain way through reinforcement. Skinner theorized that humans could learn certain behaviors in the same ways that animals could be taught certain skills.

Skinner believed that positive or negative reinforcement could be used to ingrain certain behavioral tendencies in the mind of an individual. He carried out experiments that showed that if animals were rewarded for performing certain actions, they were more likely to perform those actions again in the future, and if they were punished for performing certain actions, they were less likely to do the same in the future.

Shape Psychology

Shape psychology is also known as Gestalt psychology. It is an alternative to both structuralism and behaviorism. A discussion of the history of psychology would be incomplete if we did not at least mention it. This form of psychology was developed by several German psychologists, most notably Max Wertheimer, Wolfgang Kohler, and Kurt Koffka.

Gestalt psychology is based on the concept that the human mind's perception of objects is more than just the sum of the object's parts. This means that it is wrong to analyze the individual parts of an object because it is the wholeness of the object that gives shape or meaning to each part.

Gestalt psychology is a criticism of structuralism because it rejects the idea that a person's experiences or his consciousness can be broken down into specific elements or even individual parts. Unless the experience is observed as a whole, it would not have meaning. Gestalt psychology is also a criticism of behaviorism because it rejects the idea that only observable behavior is important in understanding psychology.

Gestalt psychology echo is the maxim that "the whole is greater than the sum of its parts." In classroom settings, Gestalt psychology is often explained using images of similar objects, which seem different based on the context of their surroundings. For example, if you have two dots of the same exact diameter, the one placed between smaller dots would appear to be larger, and the one placed between larger dots would appear to be smaller. In other words, our perception of an object changes depending on the context.

Modern Views of Psychology

Psychology has evolved a lot in the era after World War 2 and into the 21st century. In the 1950s, ethical standards and practices in the field of psychology were established, and some of the first drugs for the treatment of psychological conditions were introduced.

Cognitive psychology was also pioneered in the mid-1950s (we will discuss cognitive behavioral therapy at length later in this book). Even today, new insights are still being discovered in the field of psychology, and the more we find out, the more we understand what drives us as human beings.

Chapter 2: What Is Psychology Based On?

We have mentioned that psychology is the scientific study of the mind as well as human behavior. To understand human behavior, we first have to understand how the human brain works because of the fact that various parts of the brain control different aspects of our behavior. Brain functions are localized—meaning that everything that we sense, do, or think is made possible by a specific part of the brain. It is therefore fair to say that an understanding of psychology is not possible unless you first take the time to understand the anatomical structure of the brain and what each part of the brain does.

Scientists agree that the mind is not something physical that you can point to or identify, but it exists because of the collective functioning of the various parts of the brain. Therefore, psychologists seek to understand how the functions of the human brain related to the behavior of the human mind. The brain is, of course, responsible for a lot more than just the functions of the mind. It controls things like movement and even basic processes such as breathing and the secretions of hormones in the body.

When we look at the relationship between the brain and the mind, we won't go into much detail exploring all the other brain functions that aren't directly related to the mind — we will try as much as possible to focus on the aspects of the brain that are relevant to psychology.

An Anatomical Outline of the Human Brain

All animals have brains, but the more complex the animal is, the more advanced its brain is. Mammalian brains are relatively more advanced than those of other animals (e.g., reptiles), and of course, the human brain is by far the most advanced.

Less complex animals have brains that are designed to process simple survival functions. Such animals are able to survive as long as their brains remind their bodies to breathe, to eat, to take a rest, etc. However, complex animals need brains that allow them to feel things, to remember things, to make reasonable judgments, and to make certain predictions that are crucial to their survival. When an animal evolves further, new brain functions are added on top of older ones, so it's fair to say that the brain is somewhat layered in terms of the functions that it can perform. The basic brain functions that keep you alive came first, followed by the functions that help you survive and get along with others in society.

Parts of the "Old Brain"

The innermost parts of the brain are responsible for the most basic functions that allow us to stay alive, they are generic in the sense that they also exist in other animals, and they are the same as the ones that our ape ancestors had. This innermost part of the brain is commonly referred to as the "old brain." It is the part that is attached directly to the brain stem, at the point where the spinal cord joins the brain.

The medulla is at the very base of the brain stem. It controls the essential body functions, such as the beating of the heart and the breathing of the lungs. The medulla functions automatically, meaning that you do not have to remember the processes or to make a conscious effort in order to perform the body functions that are controlled by the medulla.

The pons is located above the medulla. This part helps to coordinate some of the other body functions that are automatic. The pons controls the autonomic body functions, and it also relays information between the cerebral cortex and the cerebellum. It also controls the sleep function (without it we would not know that we need rest).

The thalamus is located at what can be considered the geometrical center of the brain. It receives sensory information from all the sensory organs of the body, and it makes it possible for us to feel, hear, see and taste.

The reticular formation is a network within the brainstem that is important for arousal (in neuroscience and psychology; the term arousal refers to functions such as locomotion, sleeping, and sensing pain).

The cerebellum is also referred to as the "little brain." It is located at the bottom of the brain stem. It is a baseball-sized section that is responsible for many survival functions, such as non-verbal learning, storage of non-verbal memories, our ability to sense time, and our ability to modulate certain emotions. It stores and processes the information necessary for voluntary movement, which means that it is responsible for your ability to walk at different paces, to dance, to run, etc. Substances such as alcohol, which explains why people tend to stagger when they are drunk or on drugs can affect the functioning of the cerebellum.

The parts of the brain that we have discussed are responsible for all the basic brain functions. Animals can live and survive with just the parts that we have already mentioned. In fact, reptiles have survived for hundreds of millions of years with just these components. With the "old brain", animals are able to keep all body functions running smoothly, find food and water, stay vigilant against predators, and remember to rest.

Parts of the Limbic System

The limbic system consists of the amygdala, the hypothalamus, and the hippocampus. It is like a border area that separates the old brain and the newer parts of the brain. Let us look at each of the three parts of the limbic system:

The amygdala is made up of two clusters of neurons, each of which is about the same size as a lima bean. The neurons in the amygdala are involved in the consolidation of memory, and the expression of various emotions. Neurologists have been able to elicit different emotions from mammals by stimulating different parts of the amygdala. When certain parts of the amygdala are stimulated, an animal (or a person) can elicit a highly aggressive reaction (also known as the "fight instinct"). When other parts of the amygdala are stimulated, the animal can react by cowering away or even running off (this is called the "flight instinct"). These emotional reactions are controlled by neurons in the amygdala which are so close together that even neurologists who run tests on animal brains in lab settings have to use the trial and error method to figure out which neuron clusters are responsible for which emotional reactions.

The hypothalamus is responsible for steadying certain important body conditions. It regulates your body temperature and your circadian rhythms, and it has responsible for reminding you to eat (it is the reason why you feel hungry). The hypothalamus also controls the endocrine system, especially the pituitary gland (which is located right beneath the hypothalamus).

The hypothalamus is also known as the pleasure center of the brain. It is a part of the reward center of the brain, and it can make us feel pleasure when it is stimulated in a particular way. It is important to note that the pleasure that we feel as a result of the stimulation of the hypothalamus can be addictive. In fact, the hypothalamus is one of the components of the brain that are responsible for the kind of addiction that leads to substance abuse.

The hippocampus is central to verbal learning, and the retention of memory. If the hippocampus is damaged, you can lose your ability to learn new things or to store new memories. There are many documented cases of patients who developed amnesia because of damages to the hippocampus.

Parts of the "New Brain"

The cerebrum has two hemispheres, and it makes up around 85% of the entire human brain in terms of weight. It is the most advanced part of the brain, and it is responsible for functions that distinguish humans and higher animals from lower ones. The cerebrum controls your ability to think, to communicate verbally, and to perceive things. The right and the left hemispheres of the cerebrum are connected by the corpus callosum, and each of the two hemispheres is responsible for different higher brain functions.

Even though we have a split brain with two distinct hemispheres, the corpus callosum ensures that the functions of each hemisphere of the cerebrum are closely interlinked and properly coordinated, so the brain generally functions as one. Still, largely either one hemisphere or the other controls higher brain functions. For example, you may have heard that the left part of the brain is more involved in language acquisition and speech, while the right side of the brain is more involved in certain creative tasks. It is important to note that people's creative abilities or talents are not a result of some parts of their brains being more developed than those of others are — that is a myth.

If the corpus callosum in the brain is damaged (or if it is surgically removed as a treatment for conditions such as severe epilepsy), the left and right sides of your brain will fail to communicate, and you will essentially have two brains in your head. Patients with this condition are called "split-brain patients," and neurologists have observed cases where one side of the brain is completely unaware of what the other side is doing.

The cerebral cortex is a thin layer in the brain that is made up of over 20 billion interconnected neurons that cover both the left and the right hemispheres of your brain. It is the outer layer of the cerebrum. Many psychologists consider it the most important part of the brain because it is the component that makes us human. The neurons in the cerebral cortex form "neural networks," which are responsible for enabling us to learn new things and develop memories.

Neural networks in the brain are formed when we learn to perform certain tasks. For example, as a child, you learned how to tie your own shoes. During the first few tries, you had to struggle to remember what motions you needed to follow exactly in order to tie your shoes. As you did this, neurons in your brain were firing in a specific pattern, forming the neural network that enabled you to tie your shoes. With each subsequent try, the neurons kept practicing. After practicing for some time, the neural network was fully established, so your ability to tie your shoes became automated. Today, as you dress up in the morning, and as you put on your shoes, you probably do not even stop to think about it. The reason you are able to tie your shoes, button your shirt, and perform lots of other routine activities without giving it much thought is because the neurons in your brain are working together as well trained teams (neural networks) to make it possible for you to do everything that you do on autopilot.

The cerebral cortex is made up of 4 main lobes, namely the frontal lobe, the parietal lobe, the temporal lobe, and the occipital lobe. Fissures separate the lobes. Since the cerebral cortex covers both hemispheres of your brain, you have two of each kind (one on the right and one on the left). Each pair of lobes have their own set of unique functions.

The frontal lobes are responsible for your ability to speak, your ability to make judgments in different situations, your ability to make plans, and your ability to think in an abstract way. The frontal lobes are also responsible for aspects of your personality.

The parietal lobes receive and process information about your sense of touch, as well as information about the position of your body.

The occipital lobes do process information related to your sense of sight.

The temporal lobes, which are located at the back of the brain, receive and process information related to sound. They make it possible for you to comprehend speech.

Other smaller regions in the cerebral cortex have specialized functions. For instance, the motor cortex is located at the end of the frontal lobe, and it controls your voluntary movements by sending messages to the body, which makes it possible for you to perform functions such as picking up objects. The somatosensory cortex is located right after the motor cortex, and it processes physical sensations. It is the part of the brain that tells you if a surface you are touching is rough or smooth.

The lobes of the cerebral cortex have "contralateral control" over the senses for which they are responsible. That means that they control signals from the opposite side of the body—for example, your left occipital lobe does process information from your right eye and vice versa.

Glial cells are billions of cells that surround the neurons in your cerebral cortex. They provide support, nourishment, and insulation for your neurons, which means that they are responsible for keeping your neurons alive and stopping your brain from degrading.

We have mentioned that the cerebral cortex is the most important part of the brain for psychologists because it is responsible for our ability to learn and to modify our behavior. It is where our thought processes occur, and where our memory recollections take place. If Wilhelm Wundt could understand the structure of the brain the way we do today, he would probably argue that the cerebral cortex was the location of the conscious mind.

It is important to remember that even though aspects of our conscious mind are not physical, the anatomical makeup of the brain is still closely linked to our psychological state. For instance, if you had an injury on a specific part of your brain, you could lose certain memories that are important to your psychological makeup, and integral to your personality. There are documented cases where people with brain damage have exhibited major shifts in their personalities. This serves as evidence that proves that an understanding of brain anatomy is central to our understanding of human behavior. You cannot have one without the other.

Chapter 3: How Do We Think and Remember?

In the human brain, thinking and remembering do work in ways that are somewhat similar to each other because they both involve the use of neurons and the establishment of neural networks. In some cases, these two processes may even be intertwined. For example, when you are trying to do some mental math, you first have to remember the formulae involved in the calculation and then think through the calculation process before you have your answer. In this chapter, we will go into details and discuss how the human brain thinks, as well as how it stores and retrieves memories.

How Does the Brain Process Thought?

We have mentioned that the brain contains cells that are known as neurons. These neurons are connected to each other with long and thin "arms" which are referred to as axons so that the neurons form what looks like a vast web of cells that are linked to each other. When you think, the neurons in your brain fire up, and they shoot signals across the brain from one cell to the next. These processes require a lot of energy. Although the brain only makes up 2% of the body mass, it uses about 20% of all the energy that your body burns. Thinking and other brain processes that require the firing of synapses are made possible by the presence of glucose in the bloodstream.

When you start thinking, the brain cells involved in that particular thought process will use a special protein to absorb glucose molecules through their membranes. Those cells then use the energy from the glucose to send signals to other cells within the network, making it possible for you to carry on with the thought process. Signals are sent from one cell to the next using electrical charges. The electrical charges in your brain are different from the electricity that you use to power your devices at home. Brain electricity is in the form of ions. If you remember your chemistry, you know that ions are molecules that have a charge.

One neuron will send a charged ion along the length of its axon. When the ion gets to the end of the axon, it changes into a chemical signal that is referred to as a "neurotransmitter." The neurotransmitter is kept safe in a "vesicle" so that it is not lost or destroyed. The space between two neurons is called the synaptic gap. Neurotransmitters inside vesicles are released from the axon into the synaptic gap between the cell where the signal originates and the cell where the signal is being sent. As the neurotransmitter crosses the synaptic gap and reaches the axon of the receiving cell, it is again turned back into an ion, and it moves along through that neuron until the signal is again sent to the next neuron using the same process. This whole process is made possible by ATP (adenosine triphosphate) molecules, which are produced by the mitochondria when it burns glucose.

Have you ever had brain fog? That is when you are trying to think hard to understand something, but you are unable to, or the brain just feels a bit slow and hazy. There are several possible causes for this, one of which could be fatigue. However, if it is still early in the day and you experience this, the more likely explanation is that there is a shortage of glucose molecules in your bloodstream, so your brain cells are not getting the energy they need to send out or to receive signals from each other. A small snack may be just what you need to fix your brain fog.

Have you noticed that thinking through complex concepts is difficult when you are learning them for the first time, but it gets easier after you have already done it several times? Well, there is a scientific explanation for this. We have talked about the existence of neural networks, which make it possible for the brain to learn all kinds of things. These neural networks are also useful in the thinking process. To understand how they make it easier for you to think about concepts that you are already familiar with, let us use the analogy of houses within the same neighborhood.

Imagine that there are two houses built in close proximity to each other. In the beginning, there are no footpaths between these two houses. You move into one of the houses, and a neighbor moves into the other. One day, you walk across to the neighbor's house to chat. You become friends of sorts, and you keep going over to say "hi" every day. From the first time that you go over, a footpath starts to form on the ground on which you walk. With subsequent visits, the footpath becomes more established. After the footpath is fairly established, you might even decide to pave it and make it a permanent thing. That is how neural pathways in the brain are established. The more often certain pathways are used, the more developed them because, and the easier it becomes for you to use them in the future.

Do you remember the first time you went through the thought process of calculating the tip that you had to leave after you had dinner at a restaurant? You may have had to strain a bit then, but now, your 'mental math' is much better because the pathways involved in that kind of thought process are more established because you have done the same thing lots of times over the years.

How Does Our Brain Store and Retrieve Memories?

Memory as a concept has many aspects to it. There is the recognition aspect of memory which you activate when you see someone's face and remember who they are, or when you look at a fruit and remember what kind of fruit it is. There is the recall aspect of memory that you use when you remember whether it rained yesterday. There is also the aspect of procedural memory, which you use when you have to remember how to perform complex functions.

In many scientific disciplines, human memory is defined as information that has been stored in the brain and may be recalled (recollection may be problematic in cases of brain damage or repression). Memory can also be defined as learning that has persisted over a certain period. Memories are not just about information — they are also about subjective information such as emotions and feelings.

From a psychological standpoint, memories can be retrieved by either recalling, recognizing, or relearning. We have already given examples of recollection and recognition. You recognize something when you have a sensory encounter with that thing or something that is similar to it. When we talk about recognition, it is easy to assume that it is only about the sense of sight, but it is more than that. A sensory encounter could be the taste a particular drink, the smell of a certain type of food, the feel of a certain surface, or the sound of a certain bird.

Recalling is often used to retrieve factual and experiential memories. You may need to recall information you learned in school, experiences that you had in the past, or a list of things that you need to pick up from the supermarket on the way home.

Relearning is also a key way of retrieving a memory, especially when you are dealing with memories about complex concepts. It may seem odd, but you can actually retrieve a memory by learning the information contained in that memory afresh. In fact, relearning is considered to be a quantifiable way of retrieving a memory. For example, if you take a whole hour to study one chapter of a book for the first time, you may be able to quantify how much of it you remember by measuring the amount of time it would take you to relearn the information within that chapter. If you are in school, the time it takes you to learn a concept for the first time would typically be longer than the time it would take you to relearn it as you revise for your end terms because as you do it the second time around, you are actually being aided by your memories.

So, how does the information that enters your brain turn into memory? In theory, 3 stages are involved in turning information into memories. First, the information is encoded into the brain. Second, it is stored in the brain for future use, and third, it is retrieved when the need to remember arises. Memories are stored in the brain in two different ways—for a short time span, or for a long term span. Memories are therefore categorized into short term and long-term memories.

Long-Term and Short-Term Memory

Short term memory is important because it makes it possible for us to perform all kinds of tasks. Without short term memory, you would not be aware of the things that are going on around you, and you would not be able to perform ordinary tasks to completion. Your whole existence would be a confusing blur. Theoretically, you also won't be able to create long-term memories if you didn't have short term ones—that's because long-term memories are actually created from short term ones. If the brain detects that certain short-term memories are crucial, it will convert them into long-term memories.

We talked about the hippocampus when we discussed the anatomical structure of the brain. That is the part of the brain where short-term memories are stored and played back. The hippocampus takes a series of sensory memories that are somehow related, and it links them by creating connections between neurons to form neural networks. the neural networks aren't immediately fixed in place — the more important a memory is deemed to be, the harder the hippocampus works to fix its corresponding neural networks in place, so the more likely it is to be set in the brain as a long term memory. The manner in which the neural networks are fixed in the brain creates some kind of index that can be used to access various memories.

People tend to compare the way the human brain stores memories to the way that computer systems do. However, with the brain, there is no central place that can be considered a "hard drive" or a "server." Memories are stored in a biological mess of interconnected neural cells.

Furthermore, memories (both short term and long term) are aggregated in the brain on a molecular level. That means that the capacity of the human brain to store information is virtually limitless. The brain has enough molecules to store much more information than you do would ever be able to acquire in your lifetime. However, the fact that memories are aggregated at a molecular level also comes with a downside. The brain is organic and carbon-based, which means that some of the molecules can degrade and break down over time. When molecules in the brain are degraded, your long-term memories either can vanish or are modified in certain ways. That explains why our memories of events tend to change over long periods, and why we tend to forget small details and only remember things in broad strokes. As we learn new things, the brain keeps rewiring itself in order to store the new incoming information, and this can modify our older memories.

So how do we forget? Well, scientists do not fully understand whether 'forgetting' results from the deletion of memories, or whether those memories are just lost or misplaced somewhere in the brain. Some have theorized that the human brain cannot truly forget a memory and that when you cannot remember something, it is just because your mind is unable to access that memory in the brain index. Lost memories can sometimes be recovered through forms of therapy such as hypnosis.

Chapter 4: Why Emotions Influence Our Psychological State

The first thing you need to understand about emotions is that they are controlled by the brain and not by the heart. This feels like something that should be understood, but you may be surprised by how many highly educated people still infer that emotions are "matters of the heart." In your life, someone has probably told you to "follow your heart" or to "listen to your heart." This advice may even have seemed useful when you had to make decisions about your career or your personal relationships. Our intention is not to turn you into a robot, but if you want to reap the benefits that come from understanding psychology, you have to remember that all emotional reactions are controlled by the brain (even those emotions that make your heart race).

As far as the various types of emotions are concerned, different scholars have often disagreed about which emotions can be considered as basic emotions and which ones should be categorized as secondary. Most psychologists subscribe to Robert Plutchik's theory, which claims that there are essentially 8 basic emotions and that the rest of the emotions are secondary because they are closely related to one or more of the basic ones. According to this theory, the basic emotions include:

- Fear is defined as the feeling of being frightened, scared, or afraid.

- Anger is defined as the feeling of being enraged or angry.

- Joy is defined as a feeling of happiness or gladness.

- Sadness is defined as the feeling of being sad. It can also take the form of sorrow or grief.

- Surprise refers to the emotion you feel when you are unprepared for some form of sensory stimulus.

- Trust is a positive emotion that you feel towards someone or something. Admiration is considered a stronger version of trust, while acceptance is thought to be a weaker version of trust.

- Anticipation is the feeling that arises from looking forward to something in a positive way. The expectation is similar to anticipation, but it has thought to be a more neural emotion.

- Disgust is the feeling that something is nasty, wrong, or taboo.

It may seem odd, but even the most respectable psychologists find it hard to come up with a standard definition for the term "emotion." Emotions encompass many things, which is why if you spend a lot of time reading psychological journals and books, you may come across close to 100 definitions of "emotion" that vary slightly from each other. So, before we attempt to define the term, let us discuss the various components of emotion.

Components of Emotion

A proper definition of emotion should mention something about the way a person feels when they are emotional. The 'feeling' aspect is important in helping to identify specific emotions and in trying to gauge the magnitude of those emotions. There is also a physiological component to our emotions. That refers to the bodily reaction that is the basis of the emotional feeling that one experiences. A definition of the term 'emotion' should also consider the effects that emotions have on people's perceptions, on the way we think, and consequently on the way we behave. Another important aspect of emotion is how it drives or motivates us towards taking certain kinds of action. There is also a component of emotional expression. That refers to the way we show specific emotions through verbal language, gestures, and facial expressions. Now that you see how complex the term "emotion" is, you may be able to understand why psychologists shy away from one-sentence definitions.

Still, we let us look at a couple of definitions that have tried as much as possible to encompass all the aspects that we have just talked about:

One common definition states that emotions are reactions, which consist of "subjective cognitive states, physiological reactions, and expressive behavior." In this context, the term "subjective cognitive state" implies that there is a personal aspect to emotion (meaning that emotional reactions to similar stimuli may differ from person to person). The term "physiological reactions" refer to physical and chemical changes that occur in our bodies when we experience emotions (for instance, your heart rate, body temperature, blood pressure or hormonal concentrations could change because of emotional reactions). The term "expressive behavior" in this case refers to the outward signs that we show as a result of internal reactions that we experience when we feel certain emotions (for example our faces, body positions, or states of motion could change when we experience certain emotions).

Another much shorter definition of emotion, which many psychologists find acceptable, is that emotions are "feelings that in general, have both cognitive and physiological elements, and they influence behavior."

Theories of Emotion

There are many theoretical explanations of how and why we experience emotions. Psychologists have often had different explanations for emotional processes, but for our purposes, we will look at four of them. understanding theories of emotions can help you better understand how emotions act to influence our psychological states, and what we can do to regain control over emotions that may have detrimental effects on our lives, our relationships, and even our careers. Here are 4 theories of emotion that you need to know about:

The James-Lange Theory of Emotion

This theory is based on the hypothesis that the emotions that we experienced are based on our perceptions or interpretations of the physiological responses that we experience as a reaction to trigger events. That is a long and winding sentence, so let us break it down to make it easier to understand. The theory is that when trigger events occur, our bodies respond to those events, and then we interpret the bodily responses and produce outward emotional reactions based on those interpretations.

Let us use a real-world example to explain the James-Lange theory of emotion. If you are walking down the street and you see someone you like but have not seen in a while, you feel happy. According to this theory, the first thing is the trigger event, which in this case is seeing the person in question. The second thing that happens is a physiological response, which could be an increased heart rate. The third thing is your interpretation of your physiological reaction, which in this case is you associating your increased heart rate with the emotion of happiness. The fourth thing is the outward expression of the emotion, which could be you smiling at your friend.

What makes this theory different from others is the argument that it is your awareness of your physiological response that causes the emotion, and not the trigger event itself. Many psychologists find this theory somewhat problematic because of this implication. For example, when one experiences pain, one possible physiological reaction would be to cry, and the emotional reaction would be to express sadness. If we were to follow the logic of this theory, we would conclude that one does not cry because she is sad. Instead, she becomes sad because she cries.

If the emotional reaction results from the physiological response and it has nothing to do with the trigger event, then why it is that different emotional reactions could be linked to the same physiological response? A response such as an increase in heart rate could cause happiness in the example we have discussed, but it could also cause fear, say if you were walking down the lane and you spotted a snake in the grass. Therefore, even though this theory gives many insights that can help us understand emotions, some psychologists have discounted it.

The Cannon-Bard Theory of Emotion

This theory sprang up as an alternative explanation of how and why we feel certain emotions. The hypothesis behind this theory is that when trigger events occur, we experience both emotions and physiological responses simultaneously.

If we were to return to our example of bumping into a friend as you walk down the street, under the Cannon-Bard theory, the first thing would be the trigger event, which in this case is seeing your friend. However, in this case, the two reactions that follow the trigger event would occur at the same time, meaning that you would experience a physiological response of an increased heart rate and the emotional response of happiness at the exact time without one causing the other.

This theory implies that emotional reactions are independent of physiological responses, and that can serve as an explanation of why the same physiological response may occur alongside different emotions.

The Schachter-Singer Theory of Emotion

This theory is based on the hypothesis that when we encounter trigger events, we experience physiological responses, and then we identify the reason for those physiological responses before we produce an emotional reaction to the event.

Using our earlier example of walking down the street and meeting a friend, under this theory, we can assert that the process starts the same way it does in the other cases, with a trigger event, which would be spotting the friend in question. The second step would be a physiological reaction, which in this case is an increased heart rate. The third step is what makes the Schachter-Singer theory different from the other. Here, the theory implies that your brain would identify the reason for your physiological response before assigning an emotional reaction to it. This means that the brain would make a note of the increased heart rate and associate it with the trigger event of seeing your friend, before deciding that the appropriate emotional reaction for those combined pieces of information would be to show happiness.

Unlike the first theory, this one explains why the same physiological reaction can be linked to more than one emotion. Because the brain has to link the event and the physiological response before assigning an emotion, it makes sense that an increase in heart rate combined with the sight of an old friend could cause a happy emotional reaction, while an increased heart rate combined with the sight of a snake could cause a fearful emotional reaction.

The Lazarus Theory of Emotion

This theory states that when we experience trigger events, our brains first appraise the events, before producing both emotional reactions and physiological reactions. If we were to use the same example as before, if you walk down the street and see an old friend, your brain will first assess that event and label it as both exciting and positive. Based on that label, you would then experience the physiological response of an increased heart rate and an emotional reaction of happiness at the same time.

Unlike the other 3 theories we have discussed, the Lazarus theory is the only one that accounts for the differences in both physiological responses and emotional reactions that different people experience when they face similar trigger events. Some differences in emotional reactions could be explained by personal experiences, situational factors, or even cultural contexts. The Lazarus theory implies that you can learn to control both your physiological responses and your emotional reactions, which is why it is more plausible than most other theories out there.

All the theories of emotion can be helpful to you if you are trying to figure out how to overcome the kind of negative emotions that can impair your judgment or performance in important situations.

It is a fact that the same trigger can elicit different reactions and responses in different people. Let us look again at the example of someone walking along a path and spotting a snake in the grass. None of the emotional reactions and physiological responses that the person might exhibit are set in stone. They all can be modified depending on a number of factors. If that person lives in a Western country and has had no experience handling snakes, he would most likely experience an increase in heart rate, and he would express fear. What if that person lives in an Asian country where snakes are considered special delicacies? He might have a completely different reaction, both physiologically and emotionally. He might even express joy at the sight of the snake!

Functions of Emotions

From an evolutionary perspective, emotional reactions are very important for your survival. Most psychologists agree that emotions have three main functions. The first function of emotion is that it prepares us for action. This is easy to understand. Let us say that you are walking out in nature, and you see a mountain lion staring at you from a considerable distance. Emotionally, you are going to be scared and afraid. That fear is important because it is essentially meant to prepare you to run away as fast as possible. If you do not experience fear, you might hesitate when it comes to taking action, and this would increase your chances of being mauled.

The second function of emotion is that it helps shape our future behavior. Think of a child who gets a new bike for his birthday. The child accidentally leaves the bike outside, and it is stolen. The child would feel sadness, grief, or sorrow. These are nasty emotions to have at that young age, but they serve a very important purpose because they shape the child's future behavior. When that child grows into a teenager, he would be less likely to leave his laptop unattended in a public place. When he rents his first apartment, he is less likely to leave the door unlocked as he goes out for a walk. Whenever he is close to doing something negligent, the memory of the sad emotion he experienced as a result of careless behavior will help him make a better choice at that moment.

The third function of emotion is to regulate the way we interact with each other socially. It is not just about our own emotions—it's also about the emotions of those around us. Being mindful of other people's emotions makes it possible for us to coexist. That is why outward emotional expressions are very important. You can be able to tell if a friend is sad, and you can offer her some kind of support. You can tell if your boss is angry on a particular morning, and this helps you avoid doing something that could cause you to be verbally lynched. If people did not express emotions, our societies would be a lot more chaotic, because we would be offending each other without realizing it.

Controlling One's Emotional Reactions

We can control our emotions by changing the way we perceive and appraise the trigger events for those emotions. That technique has very many variations and applications, and it is widely used in different types of therapies, e.g., in anger management. For this technique to work, it's important to realize that you actually do have a lot of control over your own emotional reactions. In the next chapter, we will talk about emotional intelligence, and we will have further discussions about how you can be more in control of our emotions.

Chapter 5: How Emotional Intelligence Is Related to Psychology

Psychologists define emotional intelligence as one's ability to identify, comprehend, and manage his or her own emotions, as well as the emotions of other people in his or her surroundings. In other words, if you have high emotional intelligence, it means that you have perfected the ability to know how you feel at any given time, to tell what your feelings mean, and fully to understand the effects that your own actions and emotions can have on the people around you.

Emotional intelligence is abbreviated as EI, and it is important in every walk of life. If you are a political or business leader, you need emotional intelligence to succeed in your leadership duties. If you are an educator, EI helps you understand your students a lot better, and it makes you more effective at your job. If you are a parent, EI can help you understand the challenges that your kids are facing, and it can help you nurture them and help them grow up to be more emotionally balanced. In your career, EI can help you stay calm and in control when situations get challenging and it can help you advance a lot faster than others who may even be smarter than you in terms of traditional IQ metrics. In your relationship, having high EI helps you understand the needs of your partner a lot better, and it can help you have a happier and more fulfilled relationship.

Psychologists agree that emotional intelligence has five major components. These components include self-awareness, the ability to self-regulate, motivation, the ability to empathize with others, and other general social skills.

The Element of Self-Awareness

The first component of EI as we have mentioned is self-awareness. The state of being self-aware means that you have the ability to know how you feel and to know what your feelings mean. It also means that you are aware of the effects that your actions have on everyone in your life. Self-awareness does not mean being vain or being obsessed with your own positive traits. Instead, it means that you have a clear picture of your own strengths and weaknesses when it comes to emotional issues. To be self-aware in an emotionally intelligent way, you have to make sure that you know what kind of person you are exactly. Are you quick to anger? Do certain issues make you sad or depressed? Do you fall in love too fast?

Being self-aware is like having a blueprint of your own psychological makeup. In order to develop self-awareness, you have to document your own emotional journey and revisit it to gain an understanding of the triggers that elicit certain emotional reactions in you. One way to accomplish this is by keeping a journal of your emotions. Writing down your thoughts and your memorable experiences during any given day can boost your self-awareness.

At the end of the day, you can sit down on your computer or take out your journal and try to recall all the notable emotional reactions that you had during that day. Did you yell at someone? Did something scare you to the point of paralysis? Did something disgust you, surprise you, or make you extremely happy? You need to consciously process and analyze these reactions to figure out your own emotional strengths and weaknesses.

You can also increase your self-awareness by slowing down and processing your strong emotional reactions in real time. That means that when you feel a strong emotion as you go by your daily activities; take a moment to look at that situation from several angles. If a colleague annoys you at work, and you feel your level of anger is rising, you can take a minute to analyze that situation, and try to figure out what it is within you that is making you react in the specific way that you are reacting.

Nurturing Your Ability to Self-Regulate

Being emotionally intelligent means that you do not lash out or overreact when you find yourself experiencing certain emotions. That means that when you find yourself in situations that have the potential to flare up your negative emotions, you have to be able to tap into a source of power inside you to fight the desire for that kind of emotional reaction.

How can you learn self-regulation? Well, first you have to know your weaknesses and figure out ways to reduce them. If you have already started up on improving your self-awareness, you can come up with a list of your triggers and other things that contribute to your worst emotional tendencies. Then you have to set practical rules for yourself and to create "scripts" that can guide how you go about reacting to certain situations.

Let us say for example that you often get into emotionally charged arguments with your colleague. When you have time alone at the end of the day, you could think about conversations that ended with angry exchanges, figure out the lines that you crossed which led to an escalation of the situation, and then set rules for yourself about lines that you will not cross again in the future.

It is possible to regulate your emotions by deciding how you will react to certain kinds of situations before you find yourself in those situations. If you decide that you will not use curse words anymore, you are less likely to throw them at people when you get into arguments

.

You can also regulate your emotions by teaching yourself to take responsibility for your negative emotional reactions and to become more accountable. Whenever we have negative emotional interactions with other people, we find it very easy to see the fault in their actions. However, the truth is that it takes two to tango. Even if somebody is taunting you, you still have control over how you are going to react to his offensive actions. This also applies to emotions such as fear. If you have a fear of public speaking, you have to remember that you can control that fear if you learn to regulate your emotions. Self-regulation is about holding yourself to a higher emotional standard than the people around you.

The Component of Motivation

Motivation is the component of emotional intelligence that can make you even more successful than people who are smarter than you are in the classical sense of the word. If you find ways to reduce your negative emotions and to channel your positive emotions towards keeping you motivated, you can succeed in pretty much anything, be it your career, your personal life, or your effort to improve your mental and physical health.

To stay motivated, you have to revisit the emotional foundations that lead you to take up a certain activity. For example, if you started a fitness program, and things start getting difficult, remind yourself about the negative emotions you were trying to get rid (e.g. sadness and lack of self-confidence), and what positive emotions you were hoping to enjoy as a result of that decision (e.g., happiness and confidence). When you re-examine those emotional foundations that led to your decision, you may be able to find the motivation that you need to carry on with difficult or complicated tasks.

When you are faced with failure in some of the things that you do, you should find ways to change your perception of such situations. Instead of feeling negative emotions such as fear, anger or despair, you can at least feel neutral emotions such as acceptance, and try to work from there to see the brighter side of things. If you let negative emotions in and allow them to stay with you for long, you could end up on a downward spiral that would reinforce small failures and turn them into larger losses.

The Ability to Empathize

As we have mentioned, a big part of emotional intelligence is the ability to perceive the emotions of others around us properly and being able to help them through those emotions so that everyone can have a more positive emotional experience. Empathy is important in all areas of life because it makes it possible for us to relate with others, and it makes us care more about each other and coexist.

You can improve your capacity for empathy by putting yourself in other people's positions. We all have a point of view, and the fact is that we are all inherently biased in the way we view most things. When something happens to us, or to members of our families, it feels more real and more impactful than when it happens to other people. We can build empathy by mentally placing ourselves in others' shoes. Even if you are on opposite sides of an issue, you can try to see where the other person is coming from, and you can acknowledge the challenges that he is facing.

One way to develop your capacity for empathy is by paying attention to other people's body language. If we want to empathize with others fully, we cannot completely rely on their verbal communication. If you are a teacher, a student may claim to be okay because he has not developed the emotional intelligence that he needs to communicate more openly. However, if you learn to pay attention to body language, you may notice that the student is troubled, and you may be able to talk to him and figure out what personal issues he may be going through.

You should avoid being dismissive of other people's feelings. Just try to remember the last time someone dismissed your feelings—it must have felt horrible. It would be best to make your subordinates at work, if you have any, feel more appreciated. If your partner raises an issue that is important to him or her, no matter how small the issue may seem, you should understand that it is valid and important to them, and the worst thing you can do is dismiss it or fail to address it.

Emotional Intelligence and Social Skills

Social skills are a vital part of EI. For you to be considered emotionally intelligent, you must hone your core social skills which can help you fit in better with others and even take up impromptu leadership roles in social situations. Skills such as conflict resolution, communication skills, and the ability to deliver positive compliments can go a long way in boosting your emotional intelligence. Many of the soft skills that help people advance their careers and improve their personal lives are based on the ability to master one's own emotions.

Chapter 6: Psychology and Relationships

You know that healthy relationships are based on mutual love for one another and that love is one of the most important human emotions. We think of love as a single emotion, but in reality, it is more of a complex amalgamation of lots of other emotions. When you love someone, you are joyful when they are around, and you are sad when they are gone. You are anxious about your future encounters with them, and you are angry when they do things that disappoint you. Collectively, these emotions constitute love. From a psychological standpoint, you can improve your relationships, romantic or otherwise, by figuring out ways to reconcile your emotions with those of your partner. This is known as "emotional engagement," and it can be used to improve all sorts of relationships.

In this chapter, we will look at emotional engagement in romantic relationships and discuss psychological techniques that you can use to improve your relationship with your partner, even if you do not have any professional training as a psychologist. If you have proper emotional engagement within your romantic relationship, that relationship can be a source of great fulfillment for the both of you, and you will be able to lead a happier and more fulfilled life as a result.

In romantic comedies, and in pop-culture in general, we are led to believe that people have innate (almost mystical) connects, that they are meant for each other and that once they get together, they live happily ever after. Psychologists agree that there are certain qualities that attract us to our partners. However, these qualities do not guarantee success in relationships. Relationship success takes hard work, dedication, and a willingness to learn, to improve, and to tolerate each other. You have to learn how to engage with your partner emotionally, and you have to be willing to put in the work if you want your relationship to stand the test of time, and to bring forth happiness.

How to Emotionally Engage with Your Partner Using Psychological Techniques

When it comes to relationships, being emotionally engaged means creating an atmosphere where the both of you can have deep and honest discussions about the important issues in your relationship, and where everyone in that relationship feels heard. It's about creating a dynamic where no matter how difficult or complicated the situation gets, you can talk through it and resolve the issue without one of you causing the other to feel stressed. Emotional engagement is only possible with good communication, so if you want to improve how you engage with your partner emotionally, you have to nurture your communication skills as a couple.

Before you can emotionally engage with your partner, you first have to be in touch with your own emotions. You have to identify your real feelings. Figuring out your own emotions is more complicated than it sounds. Sometimes, our own emotions are mixed up, and we have to dig deep to understand how we feel about certain things.

For example, sometimes negative emotions such as anger and sadness may be mixed up in our minds, and to figure out the core emotion in that case, you would have to look at the trigger events that are causing those emotions. Supposing your partner walks into the room and tells you she has to go on a two-week work trip, starting the next morning. What emotion are you going to feel? You may feel angry that she didn't tell you early enough, but if you examine the root of that anger, you may find that you are concealing feelings of sadness that you are going to miss her, or maybe you are worried that spending that much time apart may put a strain on your relationship. That is what we mean by identifying your feelings. Emotions can be layered like onions, so you must peel off the outer layers to get to the core.

Once you have identified your true feelings and emotions, you have to share them with your partner. The two of you have to set a framework that allows each person to speak from the heart. When the two of you have heart-to-heart conversations, your whole relationship dynamic will improve because your brain has the ability to pick up nonverbal cues that indicate when your partner is honest and truthful. Couples have to learn how to share their true emotions, and the more they practice doing it, the better they become at doing it.

Our societies have certain expectations when it comes to how we behave in relationships, and if you want to communicate well with your partner, you need to get past those expectations. For example, many societies expect men to conceal their emotions, so it can be difficult for a man to open up about his true feelings in a relationship. Similarly, many cultures tell girls not to be "nags" or "high maintenance" if they want to get along with a man, so they too may be inclined to conceal their emotions to avoid being perceived as such. When two people enter into a relationship, there are instant communication barriers that are set up based on preconceived societal notions. Therefore, when you start dating someone, you have to work from the very beginning to break those barriers so that you can be able to communicate properly and to share your true emotions.

Passion is important in a relationship, but unfortunately, most of the time, it tends to be manifested through negative emotion. When you have a lot of passion in your relationship, it is easy for small disagreements to turn into loud shouting matches, and that can be dangerous and unhealthy. We are not going to tell you to curb your passion, because that can be counterproductive. Instead, most psychologists advise that people in relationships should learn to express their passion using words, and not volume.

Supposing your partner develops a habit that you find slightly annoying (the most common example is a girl being in a relationship with a man who keeps leaving the toilet seat up). If you try to address the issue with passionate yelling, the other person will feel the need to get defensive and yell back, and 30 minutes later, you will be in a shouting match with so many other unresolved issues now open and on the table, and you won't be able to keep track of your conversation. However, if you learn to channel your passion, and find the right words and tone to express it, you are more likely to engage in a healthy conversation, and you may come up with an amicable solution to the issue at hand.

When you share your true emotions with your partner, you have to make it clear to him or her that you expect a certain kind of response. If you are in a long relationship, it is very easy to start taking each other's feelings for granted. Therefore, if you are actively trying to engage with your partner emotionally, you have to make sure that you each learn how to acknowledge the other one's feelings. You can learn this habit. If you share your feelings and your partner is quiet, ask him or her to respond, and make it clear that you need some feedback. You may have to pry feedback out of your partner at first, but over time, he or she will learn that you expect some kind of response, and if you are lucky enough, your partner may even start reciprocating by sharing his or her own emotions with you.

You have to realize that you cannot keep unloading all your negative emotions on your partner and expect to keep having a healthy relationship. Psychologists suggest that if you are in a relationship and you experience many negative emotions because of that relationship, you need to find some kind of safe place outside of the relationship so that you can vent.

For example, if you are particularly angry with your boyfriend, it may be counterproductive to unload on him, so find a trustworthy person with whom you can talk, vent, and even seek some advice. You could talk to a close friend, a sibling or relative, a colleague at work, etc. You should not talk to just anyone and everyone; it must be someone who truly cares about you, and someone who respects your privacy.

If there is no one in your life that you trust to keep your secrets, you could hire a therapist, or if you are religious, you could talk to a spiritual counselor. The idea here is to have someone who is willing to listen to all your grievances about your relationship, however petty they may sound, without passing judgment. By venting, you will be able to release all your anger and frustration, and you will then be able to clear your mind and identify the real issues that are ailing your relationship without the fog of anger. That way, the two of you may be able to discuss your relationship issues like adults.

You should never make assumptions about your partner's feelings. You should try as much as possible to pick up their nonverbal cues because they may not readily tell you if they are having problems at work or with their family members. You can try to pay more attention to his or her nonverbal cues (their body language and facial expression) to see if he or she is emotionally troubled. If you sense that something is going on with your partner, you should ask them about it. If something negative happens to them and you know about it, try to make them open up and share the way they feel with you. After you have figured out what is going on with them emotionally, you can then steer the conversation towards helping them process their emotions, or at the very least, you can try as much as possible not to say something that is insensitive to their situation.

Try to make your dialogues deeper and more meaningful. If you have been with someone for a long time, you may get to a point where your relationship plateaus and the only talks you will be having will be logistical ones. Your partner is not your roommate, so you should monitor the kind of communication that you two are having. If you find that for several days, the only conversations you have been having are about paying the bills, doing chores, restocking the fridge, etc. then you should know that you are headed in the wrong direction. As partners, you should be able to talk frequently about the deep issues — your hopes and dreams, your fears, your passions, and your future. When you initiate deep and meaningful talks with your partner, as time goes by, he or she is going to feel the need to reciprocate, and your relationship will be better for it.

To engage emotionally with your partner, you have to learn to compromise. Somethings your emotional needs may be in direct conflict with those of your partner, so when you have deep discussions about your relationship, you will not always get the outcome that you were looking for. That means that there will be many conversations that will not end the way you want them to.

When you take steps to communicate better with your partner, you have to understand that you will not necessarily feel great after each talk. There are times when you are going to bare your heart out, and it's going to feel awkward. There are times when you will make certain demands of your partner, and this will create an uncomfortable feeling between the two of you. The thing to remember is that for you to make any kind of progress, you must be willing to endure some considerable discomfort. Those deep conversations that feel awkward at the beginning are going to feel more comfortable and normal with time, and in the end, you will have a more mature relationship.

In order to engage emotionally with your partner, you need to talk to him or her the way you want to be spoken to. From a psychological standpoint, we tend to have a lot of influence on the way people treat us and communicate with us. For example, when you address people formally at all times, they too will tend to address you in a formal manner. It is human nature to mirror the actions of the person with whom we are communicating. In the context of a relationship, that means that you can affect the way your partner talks to you by talking to them in a specific way, thus obligating them to mirror your tone.

For example, if you bring up an issue with your partner in a calm and collected tone, they are likely to respond to you in the same tone. Your partner may be at fault on a certain issue but if you start by attacking him or her, you are almost guaranteed to end up in a fight, and you will never get to the core of the issue at hand. However, if you raise the issue in a kind and clear tone, your conversation is more likely to stay within the realm of logic, and you are likely to work through the issue and make real progress.

It is important to remember that if you discover that there are serious deep-seated issues in your relationship that the two of you are unable to resolve on your own, you have to seek professional help. If there is an emotional issue that you have tried to address with your partner repeatedly, and you do not seem to be making any progress, there is a high likelihood that the issue has deep roots. Perhaps, someone who is professionally trained in the field of psychology can only fix even emanating from your partner's or your own childhood experiences, and it. Do not hesitate to suggest that you and your partner seek couples counseling. It is expected that your partner might be resistant to the idea of seeking counseling, but you may be able to convince him or her to go on one trial session and then go on from there. Couple of therapists are usually objective listeners, and they can guide both of you through some of your most complex emotional and psychological issues.

Chapter 7: Psychology and Mental Illnesses

Psychologists have had a difficult time defining mental disorders and illnesses because their understanding of different conditions keeps changing with time. You may have heard that back in the 1950s, psychologists and psychiatrists used manuals that categorized gay and transsexual people as mentally ill, but those manuals were later revised after experts were able to understand that sexual orientation did not stem from mental illness. The fact is that psychology is still in its infancy as a science, and the more we understand mental conditions, the better we are able to categorize them correctly and to find ways to deal with them.

Now, feelings and we all experience emotions like worry or sadness—but at what point do these things turn into real mental disorders? How can you tell if someone is just worried, or if he has an anxiety disorder? How can you tell if someone is just sad, or if he has a depressive disorder? Mental illnesses can be difficult to define or even diagnose, so mental health professionals use standardized manuals to figure out if the emotional disturbances that people experience are actually clinically significant, or they are just ordinary.

According to the current manual used by mental health professionals in the US, mental disorders are defined as syndromes that are characterized by disturbances in a person's emotional regulation, cognition, or behavior. The syndrome must reflect a dysfunction in the biological, physiological, or developmental processes that underline the mental functioning of the person in question to meet the threshold for a "disorder." It is important to note that normal responses to common stressors in life (for example mourning the loss of a loved one), or "socially deviant" tendencies (like having religious, political or sexual preferences that are different from those of most other people) cannot be considered to be mental disorders.

There are many misconceptions about mental illnesses and disorders which we need to dispel. The first misconception is the assumption that one is either mentally ill or that he is mentally healthy. Just like physical health, mental health exists on a spectrum. For example, you may be physically fine by all visible indications, but if you go for your annual checkup, the doctor might tell you that your cholesterol is a bit high. Before we start stigmatizing people who have certain mental disorders, we need to understand that when it comes to mental health in general, we are all somewhere in a spectrum; it is just that for most people, mental health issues do not rise to the level of clinical significance.

Another misconception we need to dispel is the common belief that mental illness is a sign of weakness. Mental strength has nothing to do with mental health. If someone has an anxiety disorder or is depressed, it does not mean that he is mentally weak. These conditions do not necessarily have an effect on whether or not a person can be smart enough to succeed in a high powered career.

Another misconception is that mental health cannot be prevented or treated. The truth is that in most cases, we may not have any say on whether or not we end up with a mental illness, but there are things we can do to preserve our mental health in general. Many mental illnesses stem from our genetic code, while some are triggered by traumatic events in our lives. However, all forms of mental illnesses can be managed through various therapies and treatments, and we can all pick up healthy habits that have the effect of improving our mental health. We can get rid of destructive mental habits and embrace positive habits like eating healthily, exercising regularly, and getting enough sleep.

Another misconception that really hurts people with mental illnesses is the assumption among the public that such people have violent tendencies. We only hear about mental illness in the news in the context of violent events, but the fact is that most people with mental health issues are not more violent than the average person. One final misconception that we have to dispel is the notion that mental illness last forever. The fact is that most mental health disorders are treatable, and even those that are permanent can be managed using medication and other forms of therapy.

Let us discuss some of the most common psychological and mental disorder:

Anxiety and Obsessive Personality Disorders

We all get anxious when we are in stressful situations. However, anxiety disorders emerge when a person's worries about certain issues become excessive and even chronic, and as a result, the person starts dreading normal everyday situations. There are many types of anxiety disorders that one can develop. Generalized Anxiety Disorder refers to a condition where one experiences a pervasive kind of anxiety on a steady basis. Panic Disorder is a type of anxiety disorder where one experiences serious and hard-hitting episodes of panic in response to the particular triggers that induce anxiety. Obsessive Compulsive Disorder is also an anxiety disorder, and it is where an individual experiences intrusive thoughts that compel him or her to act in a certain way. You may have heard of PTSD (post-traumatic stress disorder), which is an anxiety disorder that one may develop when he is exposed to terrifying events, usually involving the occurrence or the threat of grievous physical harm. Anxiety tends to occur alongside with depression in many cases, and among adults, it is twice as likely to affect females as it is to affect males.

Anxiety can be triggered by both biological and environmental factors, and it often starts out during childhood with mild symptoms. Anxiety can have a genetic component to it, meaning that certain people may be predisposed to anxiety. However, the development of anxiety is not inevitable, which means that even if you are predisposed to it, you do not necessarily have to develop it. Psychologists also believe that traumatic experiences in early childhood can recalibrate the way our bodies process fear, and it can cause anxiety.

The amygdala is the part of the brain that is responsible for telling if incoming sensory signals indicate that you should be worried, and it passes that message to the rest of your brain. We have already mentioned earlier in the book that our brain circuits are programmed early in life (remember the example of how one learns to tie his shoes). If you experienced something traumatic in childhood, your brain could be wired to be excessively sensitive to stimuli that relate to that traumatic event. For example, someone who almost drowned as a child may have heightened threat responses to sensory stimuli such as images of water bodies.

In typical cases, anxiety disorders come in the form of worries that are exaggerated and a conviction that one is going to experience a negative outcome whenever one faces an unknown situation. Anxiety disorders may be manifested through physical symptoms. Usually, one's muscles would tense—he or she would experience headaches and stomach cramps, as well as an overwhelming urge to urinate frequently.

You may be able to tell if you have an anxiety disorder if you tend to worry excessively about money, your personal health, your family's wellbeing, and your performance at work or at school. Of course, most people worry about these things from time to time, but if you find that you are always worried about them even if there is no sign of trouble in the offing, you may have anxiety, and you may need to seek help as soon as possible before it escalates.

If a person tends to have irrationally grim expectations and is convinced he will experience the worst possible outcome in every situation, he will be exhibiting a classic sign of anxiety. Anxiety disorders can also be manifested through being irritable at all times, being unable to relax, being fatigued, having insomnia, trembling when it's not cold, being shifty and twitchy, experiencing swallowing difficulties, having tense muscles, and experiencing various types of headaches.

Behavioral treatments are highly effective when it comes to treating anxiety disorders. Psychologists often design treatment regimens where people with anxiety disorders are made to face the situations that they fear, on a gradual and incremental basis, until they get to the point where they are able to overcome the source of their anxiety.

Some therapists also try to change the thought patterns that serve as the foundation of the person's anxiety. There are also drugs that can be used to control a person's anxiety, but there are no drugs that can cure anxiety. Currently, psychologists are studying meditation and mindfulness, and some have begun using them to treat and to control anxiety. People with anxiety disorders often undergo Cognitive Behavioral Therapy or other forms of psychotherapy to learn ways to cope with their anxiety.

Obsessive Compulsive Disorder (OCD)

We have mentioned that Obsessive Compulsive Disorder is a type of anxiety disorder. People with OCD have repeated unwanted thoughts, feelings, sensations, and mental images. These people engage in certain mental acts or physical behaviors as a response to those obsessive cognitions. When a person with OCD does a repeated action, it is often in an effort to get rid of obsessive thoughts. The action the person takes only provides temporary relief, and they may feel obligated to take another action soon. If the person does not take action that he or she feels compelled to take, he or she could face considerably heightened levels of anxiety. Compulsions can be disruptive to a person's life, so if one does not seek treatment for OCD, their ability to function in the workplace or in school could be greatly affected.

Other types of disorders, such as depression or eating disorders, accompany OCD. It can appear during childhood, during adolescence, or even in early adulthood. When OCD is manifested in adolescences or adulthood, it may be easier for the person to cope with it than when it is manifested in childhood. Children need to be tested for symptoms of OCD because if those symptoms are missed, the child could experience many problems during his or her developmental years, and he or she may never get to be a fully functional member of society.

OCD can be treated using both pharmacological and behavioral therapies. While one method or the other may be used in some cases, the most effective method of treatment is the combination of both methods. In recent years, clinical trials for drugs that have an effect on serotonin levels in neurotransmitters have shown positive results when it comes to reducing OCD symptoms. There are many drugs in the market, as well as others under development, and both children and adult OCD patients can take advantage of these medications (psychiatrists and psychologists can prescribe various drugs at different dosages based on their assessment of the severity of the OCD). Cognitive behavioral therapy is the most effective non-pharmacological therapy for people with OCD, and it is often used alone without being paired with drugs.

Depressive Disorders

People who have persistent feelings of sadness, who have lost the desire to engage in activities that they once found pleasurable, and who feel a general sense of worthlessness, are said to have depressive disorders. Now, everyone feels sad or depressed once in a while, but for it to be considered a disorder, it cannot be a momentary, fleeting thing. For depression to be clinically significant, it has to be a complex condition that affects one's ability to function normally on a day to day basis. Depression is sometimes accompanied by sleeping problems, changes in a person's appetite, and reduction in one's energy levels. Depressive disorders tend to change the way the brain interprets events and experiences, making those events seem more negative and grim. Depression can be treated with medication, psychotherapy, or a combination of both.

There is a 10% chance that you will develop depression at some point in your life, so even if you are not affected, it is an important matter that you need to learn about. Depression can come about as a result of social stress. For example, eon could develop depression after losing a loved one, breaking up, being fired, etc. If you experienced abuse or parental neglect as a child, your brain could set up a system that responds to depressing incidents with exaggerated sensitivity, and this could predispose you to depression.

Depressive disorders affect people's moods and thoughts, and they also have physiological effects. Depression causes pain, not just to the person experiencing it, but also to be people in his or her life. There are several forms of depressive disorders, and we will discuss a few of them in this chapter.

The first type is called **Major Depressive Disorder**. It comes in the form of a persistent mood of sadness alongside other symptoms, which affect the person's ability to do normal day-to-day activities. Such major episodes of depression may occur only once in someone's life, but in many cases, it occurs several times, and at either random or regular intervals. Depression is not just a mental condition — it can affect many other systems in your body. Research shows that major depression can actually compromise someone's immune system, which would explain why depression is often linked to heart disease.

Dysthymia or **Dysthymic Disorder** is another common type of depression. It is also commonly referred to as Persistent Depressive Disorder. It is manifested in the form of sadness and a low mood for most days, during most waking hours, and for prolonged periods of time—usually two years or even longer. In this case, the depression does not paralyze the person, but it has the effect of slightly impairing some of his or her normal functioning.

Premenstrual Dysphoric Disorder is a circumstantial form of depression that occurs at the beginning of the menstruation process and subsides a few days after the end of the menstruation process. It affects about 5 % of women who are within the reproductive age.

Postpartum Depression is a form of major depression that is triggered during pregnancy or early motherhood. It is often diagnosed in women who are pregnant or women who have given birth within less than a month.

Psychotic Depression is a severe form of major depression that comes with hallucinations and delusions. The psychotic elements (the delusions and hallucinations) may have themes that are similar to the depressive elements (for example, if one's depression is linked to certain inadequacy issues, or to the death of a loved one, the hallucinations and delusions may contain aspects of those issues).

There is also **Seasonal Affective Disorder (SAD)**, which is a form of major depression that is manifested during specific times of the year. This form of depression follows seasonal patterns, meaning that there are people who only get depressed during winters, while there are others who only get depressed during the summer, or during other seasons. When Seasonal Affective Depression occurs during winter, it could be because of the absence of natural light, and people with this disorder can be treated using natural light.

Symptoms of depression include persistent sadness, a feeling of anxiety, and a feeling of emptiness. These symptoms occur for most of one's waking hours, and for most days. That means that a mere few days of these symptoms may not rise to the level of clinical significance. There is also a strong sense of guilt and worthlessness that comes with being depressed. Depressed people lose interest in pleasurable activities, including but not limited to sex. One would find it difficult to think, remember, concentrate, or even to make decisions. One would also feel tired all the time. One may also experience sleep issues such as oversleeping, insomnia, or unintentional early morning awakening. One would experience major appetite changes, which could lead him to either gain or lose weight. Finally, one would feel a sense of pessimism and hopelessness, which could lead to thoughts of death or suicidal ideations.

So, what causes depression? Well, depression does not have one single cause. In many cases, it is caused by a combination of genetic, physiological, environmental and biological factors. Brain scans of people with depression have revealed that the brain functions of different people showing similar symptoms tend to differ. In different cases, the parts of the brain responsible for things such as thinking, appetite, sleep, mood regulation, or other behaviors, may show indications of abnormal functioning.

There may be a complex genetic link to depression. Although there is no single gene that is linked to depression, scientists understand that traits such as sensitivity to specific types of trigger events can be inherited. Depression however still occurs at a high rate in individuals who do not have family histories of depression, which implies that environmental factors also contribute to depression. Personal experiences such as being rejected, being isolated, being frustrated, or failing to achieve certain personal goals, can all lead to depression. Depression is also more likely to occur in people who do not have the emotional intelligence needed to process certain emotions. Traumatic experiences are also a major cause of depression.

Depression occurs twice as much in women as it does in men, and this is due to both physiological differences and experiential factors. As we have discussed, there are forms of depression that are exclusive to women, and that is because of hormones that are present in higher concentration in the female body than in the male body. When it comes to experiential factors, psychologists believe that women have more stressful lives because they tend to deal with issues such as juggling domestic responsibilities and careers, dealing with things like raising children, domestic abuse, etc. at a higher rate than their male counterparts, which could explain why they have higher rates of depression than men do.

Depression is one of the most highly treatable of all the mental disorders, and the good news is that even the most severe cases of depression can be treated, and the recurrence of depressive episodes can be prevented. Usually, when one exhibits depression symptoms, they should visit a physician for examination. Several medical conditions could actually cause depression-like symptoms. You might assume that you are depressed, only to visit the doctor and find out that you have certain kinds of viral infections or even a thyroid condition. If there is nothing physically wrong with an individual who exhibits depressive symptoms, the possibility of depression should then be considered.

When you seek treatment for depression, the nature of your symptoms will be analyzed, and the mental health professional would want to know about your own personal history, and your family's history with depression. With that information, he may be able to determine how severe your condition is, and he will then be able to know what kind of treatment you need. If you have moderate or mild depression, you can be treated using one or more forms of psychotherapy. They often use either Cognitive Behavioral Therapy or Interpersonal Therapy for the treatment of mild cases of depression. For severe depression, you may be given antidepressants, and you may have to combine those with psychotherapy. Sometimes, the mental health professional might recommend certain lifestyle changes including adding more physical outdoor activities to your life.

If you are depressed, there are several things that you can do to help yourself. You can try to open up and confide in others about your depression. You can try to force yourself to participate in fun activities. You can do some mild physical exercises, and try to go out more and participate in social activities. If you are in the middle of an episode of depression, you should try to postpone major life decisions, because you might find that you feel differently about those decisions once the episode is over.

Bipolarity

Bipolar Disorder is also referred to as Manic-depressive Disorder. It is manifested through severe shifts in one's mood. A person with Bipolar Disorder will experience phases of depression mixed with phases of high energy and excitement. Bipolar Disorder has very severe symptoms, and in many cases, it could lead to drastic and catastrophic actions, which could result in poor school or job performance, horrible decisions concerning one's relationships, and even suicide.

There are multiple types of Bipolar Disorders. In a type called Bipolar I, a person would experience manic episodes that would last for at least one whole week, and then they may experience depression. In a type called Bipolar II, a person would experience hypomanic episodes followed by depressive episodes.

Manic episodes are periods when a person with bipolar disorder has extremely high levels of irritability and high levels of energy. These periods usually last for an entire week. During that time, the person may have an inflated sense of self-worth, a reduced need for sleep, and a compulsion to take on high-risk activities. The person may also seem a lot more talkative, more easily distracted, and he may take up dangerous things such as sexual indiscretions, gambling, etc. without any regard for the consequences.

Hypomanic episodes are somewhat similar to manic episodes in the sense that the person exhibits high levels of irritability, as well as changes in social behavior. However, the changes in social behavior are minor, and not as extreme as those experienced in manic episodes. Hypomanic episodes last for about 4 days before they are followed by depressive episodes.

Bipolar disorder has no single cause, and in most cases, it is a result of multiple factors acting together. If you have a family history of the illness, you are at a higher risk of developing it yourself. There is no single gene that causes the occurrence of bipolar disorder, which means that the trait could be carried by multiple genes.

If you have Bipolar Disorder, or if you exhibit symptoms of the disease, you need to see a psychiatrist so that you can be given mood stabilizers and other types of medication. Even if you have a primary care physician who may be able to give you the medication you need, it is advisable to be in close contact with a psychiatrist who should keep a close eye on your condition and adjust your medication accordingly.

Schizophrenia

Schizophrenia is probably the most misunderstood mental disorder, and as a result, there is a lot of stigmatization that comes with it. People who suffer from it tend to experience a certain split from reality. As a society, we need to understand schizophrenia a lot better so that we can be able to show compassion to those who suffer from it.

Schizophrenia is a chronic condition that manifests in men in their early and mid-20s and in women in their late 20s. It can develop slowly, or it can come on quickly, but there is no singular event that causes it. It is characterized by incongruent behaviors and emotions, disturbed perceptions (e.g., hallucinations and delusions) as well as disorganized thinking.

People with schizophrenia tend to lose contact with reality, and they exhibit psychotic symptoms. They can lose the ability to focus on specific tasks, and their speech can become highly fragmented to the point of incoherence.

Schizophrenics experience different kinds of delusions. They can be delusions of grandeur, delusions of persecution and paranoia, romantic delusions, etc. They also experience hallucinations, which are sensory experiences that manifest themselves without any kind of stimulation (for example, hearing voices or seeing things that are not there).

There is some considerable genetic predisposition to developing schizophrenia, but it is also possible to develop the disease even if you do not have a family history of schizophrenia. Patients with schizophrenia may need hospice care.

Dissociative Disorders

These are disorders where a person's conscious awareness becomes completely separated or dissociated from their prior consciousness. In other words, the person's conscious mind is dissociated with his past thoughts, feelings, and memories.

There are many different types of dissociative disorders. Dissociative Amnesia is a disorder where a person has no memory of specific events, or where the person blocks out some specific information that was crucial to his or her identity. Dissociative Fugue is a disorder where a person leaves home and walks or travels around for hours or even months, without knowing his own true identity. Dissociative Identity Disorder or Multiple Personality Disorder is a disorder where a person exhibits two or more distinct personalities. Dissociative disorders can be brought on by traumatic events, and they are believed to be a coping mechanism that the brain uses to handle high levels of stress or anxiety.

Chapter 8: Cognitive Behavioral Therapy

Cognitive Behavioral therapy, simply referred to as CBT among mental health professionals, is one of the most effective forms of psychotherapy out there. It is used to treat disorders related to depression and anxiety, and it is often used to boost happiness and to modify people's dysfunctional emotions positively.

CBT is different from the traditional psychoanalysis model that was pioneered by Freud. While psychoanalysis probes into psychological wounds that people experienced in childhood in order to find the roots of their emotional conflicts, CBT is more concerned with providing solutions for those conflicts. What CBT does is that it challenges the distortions in people's cognition, and it tries to change negative thought patterns that lead to destructive behavior.

CBT is based on the idea that our perceptions and our thoughts influence the way we behave and that when we are emotionally distressed, our perceptions of our own reality may be distorted. In CBT, the basic idea is to identify negative or harmful thoughts and to make an objective assessment of whether they depict our reality in an accurate manner. If one's perception is distorted, an attempt is made to challenge and to overcome that perception using CBT strategies.

Situations Where CBT Is Used

CBT has some of the widest applications of any methods in psychotherapy methodologies. It can be used in children, adolescents, and even adults. It can also be used to help individuals, couples, families and other groups (there are even cases where business partners take up CBT in order to improve the way they work together). It is highly effective (or at least moderately effective) in the treatment of conditions such as general anxiety, depression, PTSD, stress, anger management issues, OCD, panic disorders, eating disorders, agoraphobia, social phobias, and marital issues. In some cases, CBT has been used to treat chronic pains (sometimes, chronic pain may be caused by psychological issues and not physical conditions).

If you have any of the disorders that we have mentioned and you choose to undergo CBT, you will be able to sit down with a professional, you will be taught how to identify harmful thoughts that are related to your particular disorder, and you will then be taught various techniques for establishing whether those harmful thoughts are realistic. The therapist will help you come up with more realistic thought patterns in place of your distorted ones, and he or she will help you decide on the right courses of action that you will have to take in response to triggers that often set off your disorder. You will learn through exercise, and you will acquire skills and techniques that you can use to cope with your disorder every day or until you have successfully eliminated it.

How and Why CBT Works

Although CBT principles and practices were established for the most part within the past few decades, some aspects of the practice have existed for much longer. In fact, the idea that people have a choice in the way they perceive things has existed for more than 2000 years, and it was well documented by some ancient philosophers and scholars (such as Epictetus and Marcus Aurelius). These philosophers believed that when a person perceived something, there was both an object and a subjective aspect to that perception. If you saw something, the objective aspects of that experience would be things like its physical appearance, its color, and shape, etc. and the subjective aspect would be how you react to the whole situation at an emotional level. Even though it is an old idea, which is essentially the foundational concept behind CBT.

Another foundational idea of CBT is the concept of facing one's own fears. People have known for centuries that the best way to overcome one's fears is to face them straight on. CBT applies that principle by making people go through a process where they analyze and break down the harmful thoughts, which cause their anxiety, depression, or other psychological problems. People deal with their problems by confronting them head-on instead of tiptoeing around them.

CBT also applies the idea of mindfulness, which has been a component of various Eastern religions for millennia. In the practice of CBT, people are encouraged to stay in the moment so that they can have a more conscious understanding of their own thought processes, which would allow them to challenge the negative assumptions that they typically make without even realizing it.

Even though some foundational ideas of CBT have been around for many centuries, the practice of CBT comes with many new and groundbreaking aspects, which make it one of the most effective modalities in psychotherapy. One thing that makes CBT unique is that it is highly structured, highly systematic, and highly scientific in its approach. In practice, CBT is somewhat similar to a highly structured exercise regimen — the only difference is that while physical exercise regimens build your body strength, CBT builds your mental strength and treats mental disorders.

Take the example of the CBT treatment used in people with depressive disorders. In most cases, these people are asked to write down their thoughts as soon as they experience something that upsets them. In the subsequent therapy sessions, they usually work through their recorded thought processes, and with the aid of the therapist, they would figure out the logical inconsistencies or the negative assumptions in their own thought processes, which may have caused them to get upset. They would then practice the correct thought processes in order to resolve the problem. Through repeated deliberate practice, a person with depression will start showing gradual improvements.

CBT techniques and regimens are developed using clinical science. That means that treatment packages are created based on scientific data, and then they are tested numerous times in clinical settings in order to determine how long it takes for the treatments to work, how the treatments can be tweaked to produce faster and better results, and what probable benefits people are likely to gain from the use of those treatments. Therapists are free to modify their CBT treatment sessions however they see fit (based on their professional assessments of different patients), but most treatments are based on standard basic principles, and they are not just pulled out of thin air.

Sometimes, when you go for CBT treatment, you will find that the therapist does not tell you anything that you do not already know deep within. In fact, if you stop to examine some of the things that trigger your own stress, anxiety or depression, you may be able to see on your own that you are stressing over nothing. However, it is important to remember that emotions can be more powerful than logic — that is just human nature. Even if the things you do in your therapy session may seem obvious, you should not write any of it off. These repeated exercises may not seem sophisticated or ground-breaking at the time, but they are actually very effective in rewiring your brain to prioritize logic over negative emotional reactions.

Common CBT Techniques

If you undertake CBT, you will be subjected to lots of behavioral experiments. Depending on the problem that you have, your therapist will come up with various hypotheses, and from those, he or she will formulate experiments which you would test on different occasions to find out which ones work best in your case.

For example, if you are undertaking CBT for the treatment of an eating disorder (e.g., overeating), your therapist may come up with two hypotheses, one based on self-criticism, and the other based on self-kindness. In one instance of the experiment, the therapist may tell you to criticize (or to mentally flog) yourself after you overeat, while in another instance, the therapist may tell you to be kind to yourself after you overeat. You will then record whether you felt the urge to overeat again after each of those experiments. The therapist will use the insights gained from the experiments to create a CBT regimen for you, or she may subject you to many other experiments before coming up with a single long-term regimen that works in your case.

Another common technique used in CBT is the recording of one's thoughts. Thought records are great tools that therapists use to help you challenge assumptions that lead to negative emotional reactions. For example, let us say that you have a phone conversation with your mother, and she says something critical about your life choices, your career, or your relationship. When you hang up the phone, the thought that crosses your mind is "My mother hates me." In that case, you will record that thought, and you will work through it in a future session with your therapist. In the future session, the therapist may ask you to outline reasons both for and against that particular thought. These reasons have to be as objective as possible.

As you go through the process of outlining the reasons for and against that specific thought, you might begin to realize that your mother's hurtful comments didn't come from a place of hatred, and that deep within, she is just concerned about you, or maybe she is working through her own issues. You will then have to practice coming up with thoughts and conclusions that are more balanced.

For example, the next time you hang up the phone after talking to your mother, your thought could be "My mother wants me to succeed in life; it's just that her metrics for success are different from mine."

Other techniques used in CBT include Pleasant Activity Scheduling, Situation Exposure Hierarchies, and Imagery Based Exposure. Pleasant Activity Scheduling is a process where you add a different fun activity to all the days in your personal calendar, and you make sure that you follow through with each activity. The activity in question has to be something that you enjoy, but it should not be harmful or unhealthy. Pleasant Activity Scheduling works surprisingly well in countering depression and anxiety.

Situation Exposure Hierarchies is a CBT technique where you list all the things or situations that are related to your disorder. Start with what affects you the most and go all the way, down to what affects you the least. For example, if you have anxiety about social situations, you could create a list starting with the things that make you the most anxious (e.g. asking a girl out on a date or delivering a speech in front of a large audience) and go all the way down to situations that make you the least anxious (like asking a woman for directions, or starting a conversation with a stranger in an elevator). You will then rate each item on your list on a scale of zero to ten. When your list is made, you will start at the bottom and work your way up that list, conquering each fear several times as you go, until you are comfortable with all the situations in your list.

Imagery Based Exposure is an exercise where you try to remember a trigger situation in as much detail as possible. If something happened and it set off your anger, anxiety or depression, you will be required to revisit that situation repeatedly and try to remember and analyze all the sensory details surrounding that incident. If it were a negative interaction with a person, you would have to think through everything including their facial expressions, the tone of voice, etc. The purpose of this exercise is to see the situation from different angles and to determine whether you could have arrived at another conclusion that would have been more logical.

Chapter 9: Psychology and Self-Improvement

You probably already know that psychological principles are widely applied for self-improvement purposes. If you are like most people, there are definitely several areas in your life that you would like to improve. Maybe you want to be more organized, to give up junk food, to take up an exercise regimen, to improve your performance at work or at school, or to just live a more fulfilled life. The changes that you need to make in your life are going to be difficult and challenging, and you may need to rewire your brain in order to find the willpower or the motivation to take action to make those changes. That is where positive psychology comes in. Psychologists these days do not just focus on issues that are clinically significant—these days, psychological principles can be applied anywhere and to anyone in order to realize specific self-improvement goals.

The first step towards self-improvement is self-awareness. We discussed self-awareness earlier in this book when we talked about developing emotional intelligence. If you want to be more self-aware, you have to take stock of your sensations, your thoughts, your emotions, and your behavioral patterns. The reason we find it hard to start new positive habits is that we have certain emotions, thoughts, and behaviors that we have become accustomed to, so our brains will tend to resort to those old habits and resist attempts to develop new ones. When we take stock of our current psychological state, we will be in a better position to figure out what areas need change, and why we are reluctant to embrace new habits.

You can take stock of your psychological state by keeping a journal for at least a couple of weeks, and then consciously reviewing all your tendencies and convictions to see which ones are inhibiting your ability to make progress in your life. Your goal, in this case, is to understand the things that limit you, and to identify the psychological chains that bind you, and stop you from achieving your self-improvement goals.

Ways to Improve Your Mindset

To achieve self-improvement, you first need to improve your mindset. Psychologists define the term mindset as a belief or a system of beliefs that orient the way a person approaches certain situations. Your mindset determines the way you perceive certain events and the way you select and execute a certain course of action in order to achieve a very specific goal. A positive mindset can help you see opportunities that are hidden, while a negative mindset can trap you in a cycle of self-defeating thoughts and behaviors and stop you from making any real progress.

As much as possible, you should avoid having a fixed mindset. The reason we have gone into so much detail in this book to explain the principles of psychology and the working mechanisms of the brain, is to make it possible for you to understand that the human mind isn't a fixed thing and that it can be trained to think in certain ways, resulting in certain behavioral modifications. People who do not understand the basics of psychology tend to assume that their abilities are innate and therefore their failure in certain areas of life cannot be prevented or reversed. A lot of people think that they are just "not good at math" or that they just "can't do public speaking." You have seen in this book how the brain learns, and how it processes thoughts, memories, and emotions, so you understand that you are fully capable of changing your brain has thought patterns by using repetition and reinforcement as a learning technique. You know that the brain is not a rigid thing, so you understand that you are fully capable of changing your mindset if you work hard on it.

Do not be preoccupied with perfection. To have a positive mindset, you have to be less concerned with doing things perfectly and more concerned with making progress and making gradual improvements. If you are preoccupied with doing something perfectly and eliminating all errors, you are more likely to be stuck where you are, and to be afraid of taking steps to change your situation out of the fear of committing errors.

Supposing you want to start exercising in order to improve your health and fitness. Your priority should be to get started as soon as possible and to make improvements as you go. You should not wait for the perfect conditions to get started. If you wait to find the perfect gym, the perfect outfit, the perfect instructor, or the perfect time, you may never get around to doing any exercise. The point is that perfection is an illusion, and looking for perfect conditions is just another way to procrastinate.

To improve your mindset, you need to learn patience. In most things that we undertake, it may take some time before we begin to see real results. If you have a well thought out plan and you have put it into action a few times, but you have not yet seen the results you have been hoping for, it does not mean you should give up immediately. Many people who go on self-improvement journeys expect to see instant result. If you are trying to pick up a positive habit, say for example you are trying to have a healthier morning routine, you have to understand that you are essentially overwriting years or even decades of old habits in your brain, so it may take some time before the new habit feels more natural to you.

How to Be More Optimistic in Your Outlook

To learn optimism, you have to acknowledge your pessimism. You have to consciously go through your pessimistic ideas and analyze them, then challenge all the negative assumption that you are making. When you identify your negative assumption, you may be able to see the error in the pessimistic conclusions that you are drawing. Even when we are pessimistic, we do not want to be called pessimists, but for this to work, assume that every negative thought you that have comes from a place of pessimism and not from an objective assessment of the situation.

In conflict resolutions, the two parties are often told to start by saying something positive about each other. You can apply the same trick to become more optimistic. For every situation that you find yourself in, try to have one positive thought about that situation no matter how negative it may be. Even if the positive thought does not ring true at the time, try to have it anyway. Let us say you get out of the house in the morning, and you realize someone stole your car. There may be no apparent upside to that situation, but you should try to dig deep and find one, even if it is a weak one. For instance, you can decide to think of it as an opportunity to get a new car (even if it is going to cost you). The point of this kind of exercise is not to turn you into a "blind optimist." It is to stop you from being habitually negative.

You can form the habit of searching for positive aspects in all kinds of negative situations, and you can even turn it into a little game that you play in your mind. Did your date go horribly wrong? Well, at least you had the chance to dine in a fancy restaurant. Were you fired from your job? Well, it is a chance to search for a new and perhaps even better job that fulfills you. Were you dumbed? Well, it's a chance to find someone whom you are more compatible with.

You can also think of someone you may know who always has a positive outlook, and try to imagine what they would have thought if they were in your situation. It can be anyone real (e.g., a friend or relative you admire, a historical figure, a famous person, a religious or spiritual figure, etc.) or even fictional (e.g., a character in your favorite movie, television series, book, comic book, etc.). For example, if you have to give a presentation to a group of people and your fear of public speaking creeps up, you can ask yourself "What would Abraham Lincoln thing or do in this case?" Honest Abe was pathologically shy, but he overcame his fear to deliver one of the greatest and most consequential speeches in history. If he could do that, then you could get yourself to keep it together for the duration of a PowerPoint presentation.

Finally, to become more optimistic, you must learn to practice optimism as often as you can. You have to overhaul your entire outlook in life, and you will not be able to accomplish that if you are ineffective in your approach. You must take every chance that you can to practice optimism and to sharpen your positive mindset. Your brain may be an "old dog," but from what you have learned in this book, it is fully capable of learning new tricks, as long as you keep reinforcing those lessons.

Chapter 10: How to Think Like a Champion

We all want to be champions in the things that we do. You probably want to excel in school, to be great at your job, and to have great personal relationships. In other words, we all want to be the best versions of ourselves— to be champions in our own right. But the question is, "how do you accomplish greatness?" when trying to understand the kind of drive that a person needs to overcome his perceived limits and to accomplish things that he initially thought were impossible, we often draw lessons from the world of sports. Looking at sports psychology allows us to have a deeper understanding of how one can achieve peak performance in all other areas of life.

In this brief chapter, we will look at some of the mental strategies that are often used by sports champions, and we may draw examples from various athletic fields. We will then talk about how those strategies can be adapted in other areas of life.

You have to understand that nobody is born with the mind of a champion, which means that those among us who are champions have had to learn how to be the best versions of themselves, and we can do it as well. You just need to practice to think like a champion, and with time, you will be able to feel and act like a champion.

Champions go for gold, not for silver. That means that no matter how impossible a goal may seem to be, your aim is to be the best, not just "good enough." If you are working on improving your relationship, you want to offer your partner the best version of yourself, so you should not settle for merely being able to get along.

Going for gold means being in your best possible shape mentally, physically, tactically, and technically. To get in the right mental shape, you have to make sure that you have the right thoughts, emotions, and attitudes to help you achieve whatever goal you have in mind. You need to tap into your inner strength and find ways to motivate yourself and to keep yourself focused on your goal, whatever it may be.

When we talk about being in the right physical shape, we mean having the stamina, the strength and the conditioning that is necessary to achieve your goal. If your goal is to start or to operate a successful business, stamina means being willing to work long and hard hours, and conditioning means picking up healthy habits that will enable you to have the strength to work harder than everyone else.

When we talk about being tactical, we mean having well thought out strategies that could help you outperform everyone that you are competing with. When we talk about being in the best technical shape, it means that you need to have all the technical skills that are needed to achieve whatever goal you have, and that comes from studying and practicing.

Every athlete spends countless hours practicing, but champions are more deliberate in the way that they practice. Champions structure their practice sessions to avoid burning out before the big day. They are also strategic in the way they practice in the sense that each practice session is meant to achieve something specific. To be a champion in various areas in your life, you also have practice in a deliberate way so that you can become an expert in the thing that you are trying to accomplish. If you are learning a new skill (e.g., playing an instrument, learning to use a new software program at work, etc.) you must take the time to practice.

You cannot expect to be a champion at doing anything if all you do is go through it a couple of times. In an academic setting, you should not settle for just understanding a concept — you want to master it. If you are learning algebra, you want to get to the point where you can "do it in your sleep." If you put in a little effort, you will be doing the same thing that everyone else is doing, and you will not be exceptional in any way.

When champions practice for sporting events, they try to make their practice conditions as close as possible to the actual conditions of the upcoming sporting event. You can also use this technique as you practice for whatever activity you are preparing for in order to distinguish yourself as a champion. If you are preparing to give a speech or a presentation, you can assemble a few friends and present it to them as though they were your real audience, and as you do this, make sure that you do it exactly the way you intend to do it in the official setting. If you are preparing for an exam, you can practice by finding a past paper and doing it under the same conditions as those that you will be subjected to on the actual day of the exam. With this kind of practice, when the actual event comes around, you are less likely to lose confidence, because you would have ironed out all the imperfections in your plan, and you will be able to anticipate any issues that may arise.

Champions learn to keep their level of performance consistently high so that when major events come around, no matter how high the stakes are, it just feels like every other practice session. In most of the things that we do, we all feel overwhelmed when the "big day" comes around. That is because we have not learned how to minimize the magnitude of major events by making them seem ordinary. Think of an athlete who runs short races. That athlete goes on so many sprints in the weeks and days leading up to the big event, so when that event comes around, he is not overwhelmed by the pomp and circumstance around it. It just feels normal, and no matter how high the pressure is, he will not choke.

Athletes and champions also learn to roll with the punches when they experience setbacks. Being a champion is not just about having the skills needed to win—Sit's about having the resilience to get back into action even when you face several defeats. As a champion, you will find defeats devastating, but you must have the thick skin needed to get up and get back in the game. In your career, if you have been passed over for a promotion that you have been working hard to get, you need dust yourself off and work even harder so that you are not passed over next time.

Finally, champions learn from their mistakes and losses. Champions always review their game tapes to see what they could have done better, and how they can change up strategies to ensure that they keep winning. That is what you need to do. If you get a decent grade in school, or if you made a profit in your business, that should not be the end of it. You should review your strategy to see how you could have scored more marks or how you could have made a larger profit.

Chapter 11: What You Need to Know About Dark Psychology

The term "dark psychology" is used in two different contexts. In the first context, dark psychology refers to a human consciousness construct, and in the second context, it refers to the study of that consciousness construct. For the purposes of this chapter, we will define dark psychology as the study of the human condition, in relation to the psychological tendencies of people who prey on others in various ways.

We all have the potential to victimize others, but most of us tend to abide by social norms that forbid or frown upon our darker tendencies. Because of our desire to be accepted in our communities, and because of our innate sense of right and wrong, most of us restrain ourselves. However, there are still some among us who act upon their darkest impulses, and the study of dark psychology seeks to understand why this is the case. Dark psychology analyses the feelings, thoughts, and perceptions that cause people to develop predatory tendencies.

This may come as a bit of a surprise, but psychologists believe that the vast majority of evil actions that are perpetrated by people are purposeful, they are based on rational motivations, and they are meant to achieve specific goals that make sense to the perpetrator. In fact, psychologists have found that only 0.01% of brutal human actions lack a purpose that can be reasonably attributed to either evolutionary science, or to some form of religious dogma.

With the rise of the internet, it has become important now more than ever to understand dark psychology because the internet has produced a completely new breed of predators who are looking for opportunities to take advantage of others and to victimize them. We now have bullies, stalkers, sexual predators, terrorists, ideological fanatics, and all sort of evil people who use the internet as their playground.

In the study of dark psychology, experts have concluded that criminal tendencies and other deviant behaviors lie on a continuous spectrum, and they vary according to levels of severity as well as degrees of purposefulness. This is most likely why there is a high likelihood of carrying out increasingly larger crimes as they grow older for people who start off doing petty misdemeanors in their youth.

The Dark Triad

Psychologists came up with the term "dark triad" to refer to a set of traits that lurk beneath the surface inside individuals who tend to use others to their own selfish benefits. The dark triad is made up of three traits: narcissism, Machiavellianism, and psychopathy. Narcissism is a trait found in people who tend to seek both special treatment and admiration from others. Machiavellianism is a trait found in people who tend to manipulate others to their own advantage and to the other person's detriment. Psychopathy is a trait found in people who are insensitive and callous towards others.

The dark triad traits are the foundational traits that cause some of the most undesirable behaviors that human beings exhibit. They have been found to underlie behaviors such as impulsiveness, aggressiveness, and sexual opportunism.

Sometimes it may not be easy to tell, but dark psychology is all around us. As we go about our daily lives, we may find that people or corporations are trying to manipulate us or take advantage of us in one way or another. You might even be surprised to find that you also use dark psychology to take advantage of the people around you! As we mentioned, evil acts exist on a spectrum, and the truth is that we all have a dark side. Psychologists have developed techniques to measure traits such as psychopathy, narcissism, and Machiavellianism in different people. In one such system, people are asked to rate themselves based on standardized questions, and in the end, they receive a score that essentially quantifies their dark tendencies.

The confusing thing about dark traits is that they can actually help people succeed in areas such as business. Psychologists have found that people who rate highly on the narcissism scale tend to be considered by others as more attractive, more driven towards success, or even more conscientious. Compared to the other 2 dark traits, narcissism is often considered the least harmful to other people, and some psychologists consider it the brightest (least dark) trait in the triad.

Machiavellianism and psychopathy are very harmful to others, and they are dominant in people who have hardcore criminal tendencies. It could be argued that narcissism can cause some level of harm to the narcissistic person, but the other 2 traits only cause harm to victims who are targeted by the person who exhibits those traits.

In our daily lives, we may encounter people who may try to use dark psychology to manipulate us. It is important to mention some of the techniques used by these people so that you are able to spot them should you encounter them as you go about your business. One common dark psychology technique is lying. You can tell that someone is a lair if they tend to exaggerate things, tell half-truths, etc. Another dark psychology technique is called love flooding. This is where someone readily showers you with compliments, shows you affection or tries to butter you up before asking you for certain favors.

Another dark psychology technique is called love denial. This is where someone refuses to give you attention or affection in order to get you to take a certain course of action. Another technique that is similar to love denial is called withdrawal. Withdrawal is referred to the silent treatment. It is where someone refuses to talk to you unless you satisfy a certain need that they have.

Choice Restriction is also a common dark psychology technique. It is where a person gives you options that you do not want, in order to stop you from making the choice that you actually want to make. Amazingly, this technique is used by all kinds of people and entities around you, and most of the time you will not even realize it.

Reverse psychology is also a dark psychology technique. It is where a person tells you one thing with the intention of getting you to do the opposite. It works because it irritates you to the point of deciding that you have something to prove to that person.

One of the subtlest and most complex dark psychology techniques used by individual and entities to get people to make decisions that are against their own best interest is called semantic manipulation. Companies and even politicians use this technique all the time to phrase things in ways that would allow them to explain the issues away if they caught on the lie. After they have gotten you to make certain decisions in their favor, they will refuse to keep their word, and they will often attribute the whole thing to a misunderstanding.

Chapter 12: How to Guard Against Psychological Manipulation

In the previous chapter, we looked at dark psychology and how we encounter it every day. Here, we want to give you tips on how to guard against psychological manipulation from all kinds of people, including close friends, colleagues at work, or even strangers with malicious intentions. We will start with the signs of psychological manipulation, and then we will proceed to discuss ways to stop manipulators from getting the best of you.

Signs of Psychological Manipulation

Sometimes, it can be difficult to tell the difference between the kind of social influence that is healthy and beneficial, and the kind of influence that falls under the realm of psychological manipulation. There are friends and family members who truly want you to succeed in life and to be happy, and they might try to influence you to take certain actions to better yourself. However, there are also people in your social circle, even close friend and family members, who might try to manipulate you, time and again, for their own benefit. You must be able to tell the difference between the two so that you can guard against manipulation.

One trick that manipulators may use is to try to gain the "home court advantage" over you. Manipulators will want to control the space where you meet or hang out so that they can dominate you and influence you while you are still feeling uneasy. If you meet salespeople, romantic interests, or other people who always insist on having all your interactions in their homes, cars, offices, or even in restaurants of their choosing, chances are that you are dealing with a manipulator.

Manipulators may sometimes let you speak first during interacts so that they can size you up and identify weaknesses in you that they can exploit. It is an old sales technique, but manipulators in social situations also use it. Some manipulators may even be so good at what they do, that they may use your own strengths against you.

Manipulators always distort facts to their advantage. They may do this by lying, telling half-truths, making excuses, or just by being two-faced. Manipulators tend to modify their versions of events to make it seem like it was the victim's fault. They may also withhold or disclose certain information in a strategic manner in order to elicit certain emotional reactions from you. They may also try to deform the truth, to show obvious biases in certain things, or to understate the impacts of their actions. One common example that you may encounter is a guy who keeps referring to his former love interests as 'crazy' to distract you from rumors that he may have been a bad boyfriend in the past.

Some manipulators may practice a technique called intellectual bullying. They may want to present themselves as experts on certain issues so that they can make you look dumb if you do not see things from their perspective. Such people may throw around many facts and figures to try to overwhelm and confuse you. This is a very common technique in areas such as sales and financial management. If someone tries to sell you on an idea by talking over your head, you can be certain that you are dealing with a manipulator. Even in social conversations, there are people who will keep trying to exert some kind of 'expert' power over you, with the end goal of pushing a personal agenda, or maybe just to make themselves feel superior.

Some people may try to manipulate you by exhibiting negative emotions or by increasing the volume of their voices. This can be subtle if you are dealing with someone who does it professionally (like a salesman) or it can be obvious if you are dealing with a social manipulator. These kinds of manipulators think that if they make you uncomfortable enough, you will give in and let them have things their way.

Some manipulators may try to limit the time you have to make decisions so that you do not get the chance to think too much about what you really want. They may prevail on you to make fast decisions by telling you that the window of opportunity is closing up fast, and by exploiting your fear of missing out.

Manipulators use negative humor to make you feel weak and powerless. They may make statements that are really criticisms, but then disguise them as jokes or sarcastic comments. They may say things about how you look, your professional or academic background, your cultural identity, your weight, your car, or pretty much anything about you that may be somewhat humbling. Their intention is to make you look bad, while they can pretend to be the funny guy.

Some manipulators may feign ignorance by pretending that they do not really understand what it is that you want, or that they do not notice the effects that their actions have on you. This trick is often referred to as "playing dumb," and it is very common even among family members, close friends, and colleagues. At home, your child may pretend not to know how to perform certain tasks to get out of doing his chores. If you are working on a project with a colleague, he may pretend not to be "as good as you" at handling certain responsibilities just so he could stick you with his workload.

Manipulators may also criticize and judge you on a consistent basis to make you feel as though you are inadequate and not as good as they are. The idea is to keep you off balance so that they can maintain an air of superiority over you. This is common in the workplace, but it can even occur among family members or couples. They will keep trying to make you doubt your own competence, and no matter how much you improve, the criticism will not stop. They also will not offer viable solutions to the issues that they raise, which means that their true intention is not to help you.

Manipulators will also give you the silent treatment. In the digital age, this trick has evolved to include refusing to reply to your calls and messages. The intention is to shift the power dynamic between the two of you and to make it seem as if you need them more than they need you. It is a kind of mind game where silence is a highly powerful form of advantage.

Guilt-baiting is also a common form of manipulation. Here, a manipulator may try to hold you responsible for his issues, in a way that is not at all reasonable. The manipulator will try to identify your emotional vulnerabilities or issues that you care about and try to use them against you. That way, he can coerce you into doing favors for him against your own will. There are extreme versions of guilt-baiting that may occur in dysfunctional relationships where one person may threaten to commit suicide if the other breaks up with him or her.

People also use victimhood as a form of manipulation. People can pretend to be victims in order to exploit your sense of duty, your good nature, your nurturing instinct, or your sense of guilt. They may exaggerate their personal problems, health issues, etc. This is common in relationships and within families because, in such settings, you will always feel a sense of obligation towards the other person.

How to Handle Manipulators

The first thing you need to consider when dealing with a manipulative person is your own safety. If you are in a relationship with someone and you start sensing that they are manipulative, you should be very careful because there is a high likelihood that they could escalate the situation if they see that their tricks are not working on you. You should confide in a person that you trust, and you should make plans to guarantee your wellbeing.

If the person uses tricks that involve negative emotions, make it very clear to them that you will not communicate with them if they keep screaming at you. If possible, excuse yourself politely and leave, then come back when they have calmed down. If a person keeps trying to corner you when you are alone in order to manipulate you, do what you can to avoid spending time with them alone. If they invite you somewhere, bring along a friend or two and let it be a social gathering. If that person is not a family member or a colleague, your best option may be to cut them out of your life altogether.

When conversing with a manipulative person and you get the sense that they are applying some of the tricks we have discussed, you should not get confrontational, and you should not call them out on it. Manipulative people do not like to be embarrassed in social situations, and they may retaliate in a way that hurts you even more. If it is a stranger, find an excuse to get away from them, and do not give them your contact information. If it is someone you know, set limits with them, and try to establish boundaries based on mutual respect.

Manipulative people may try to get close to you, but you should turn them down politely but firmly. If a manipulative person gets your contact information from a mutual friend and tries to call you during odd hours, do not pick up (it might be useful if you subscribe to a service that identifies callers with strange numbers), and do not accept their social media friendship requests. Manipulators may try to be friendly and charming just so that they can get a foot in the door. However, since you understand the tricks we have discussed here, you may be able to spot one coming a mile away.

We have said that calling out manipulators may land you in hot water, but you may be able to shake them off by countering their tricks with probing questions. When a manipulator makes certain demands of you, just ask them many logical questions that could help unravel their ploy. Ask them things like; whether their request seems reasonable to them, what it is you will be getting from what they are offering, and whether they would comply with the same request if the situation were reversed and you were the one asking them to make a decision that is contrary to their own best interests. Manipulators tend to gravitate towards easy marks, so if they find you to be too inquisitive, they might decide that you are not worth their time, and they may eventually leave you alone.

Finally, and perhaps most importantly, when you are dealing with a manipulative person, you should remember all your rights and you should make sure that you do not compromise on any of them. It is crucial that you remember you have a right to be treated respectfully, to choose your own priorities, to have your own opinions, to express your own feelings and desires, to decide what makes you happy, and to reject someone's request without being made to feel guilty. If someone is trying to infringe on any of those rights, they are most certainly manipulating you. You should politely remind of that particular right, and you should tell them that you would not try to take that right away from them, and they should afford you the same courtesy.

Conclusion

Thanks for making it through to the end of *Introducing Psychology: How People Think, and How They Can Be Influenced Using Psychological Techniques*. I hope that you have acquired a lot of useful knowledge about psychology that you can apply to improve your own life and to inspire those around you to do the same.

Your next course of action is to start applying the psychological principles that you have learned here in order to make yourself better at various things that you are interested in pursuing. As we have discussed in the book, an understanding of psychology can make you a better student, employee, parent, boss, or partner because you will have a firmer grasp of both the brain processes and the social dynamics that often precipitate negative outcomes, and you will know how to avoid them.

In the book, you have seen that we are all prone to negative emotions, so you should make a conscious effort to be more rational in your approach to life because this can help you overcome the kind of negativity and pessimism that leads to anxiety and depression.

Now that you know about various mental disorders and illnesses, you can be the voice of reason out there, and you can contribute towards putting an end to the stigmatization of such conditions. When you encounter people with mental issues, you should show them patience and compassion.

You should also keep seeking deeper knowledge in the field of psychology so that you can be able to understand yourself and others a lot better. Although we have introduced you to the principles of psychology in this book, there is still an ocean of information out there that could be beneficial to you—so do not just stop here. Keep reading and researching during your free time, and you will be surprised at how much better your life can get just by having a much deeper understanding of your own psychological makeup.

Finally, if you found this book at all useful, a review on Amazon will be greatly appreciated!

Made in the USA
Middletown, DE
08 May 2019